AGG
OF S

Also by Nelson Eustis —

Japan's Pacific Occupation
50 Years of Australian Air Mails
Basil Watson — Pioneer Airman
R. Graham Carey — Pioneer Airman
The Greatest Air Race
The Australian Air Mail Catalogue
The Ross Smith Air Stamp
Samoa Sketchbook (with A. J. Peake)

AGGIE GREY
OF SAMOA

NELSON EUSTIS

AGGIE GREY OF SAMOA

First published 1979
Second printing 1980
Third printing 1986
ISBN 0 9595609 0 4

Copyright © 1979 by Nelson Eustis
Typset by Modgraphic Pty. Ltd. Adelaide
Printed at Griffin Press Limited, Netley, South Australia

Published and distributed by Hobby Investments Pty. Ltd.,
G.P.O. Box 954, Adelaide, South Australia 5001

CONTENTS

ACKNOWLEDGMENTS

E. W. ("Ted") Roberts for all artwork.
Gary Fearnley for the front cover photograph of Aggie.

Ron Boland, formerly Managing Editor, The News, Adelaide, for his helpful advice.

My thanks to my friends in Samoa who have gathered information for me, specially to the Swann *aiga*, and to Aggie for her patience.

Nelson Eustis

GLOSSARY

aiga : the extended family — however remote.

fa'a-Samoa: in the ways of Samoa.

fa'atonu : adviser.

fale : Samoan house, any building.

fautasi : longboat.

fiafia : party, entertainment.

fono : meeting.

ifoga : ceremonial request for forgiveness.

kava : a non-intoxicating drink prepared from the roots of the pepper tree.

lavalava : clothing.

malae : Samoan "village square".

malaga : journey.

matai : a titled person, a chief, leader of family.

Mau : independence movement.

palolo : a sea annelid.

palusami : a delicacy made of young taro leaves and coconut cream.

paopao : canoe.

papalagi : European, white man.

pisupo : "bully" beef, corned beef.

sene : cent.

siva : dance.

soifua : goodbye.

tala : dollar.

taro : subsistence root vegetable.

taule'ale'a : untitled person.

taupou : a daughter of a high chief, the leader of the village young women, noted for her charm and good looks.

tusitala : teller of tales, story teller.

Western Samoa lies between latitudes 168° and 173° west, and between 13° and 14° south of the Equator.

It comprises the large islands of Upolu and Savai'i. Between these two islands are the smaller inhabited islands of Apolima and Manono. To the east are the islands of American Samoa.

Temperatures average 84.9° in the dry season and 74° in the wet season. Annual rainfall averages 100 inches.

Western Samoa became an independent state in 1962, as a result of a poll conducted in the country by the United Nations.

The capital of Western Samoa is Apia which is situated on the island of Upolu. Apia is also the only town and has a population of over 35,000. The total population is estimated at 160,000. Most of the people live in the many villages that are located on the coastal belts of the islands.

Western Samoa's economy is based mainly on agriculture. The three main exports are copra, cocoa and bananas. New industries such as timber, fishing and tourism are being rapidly developed.

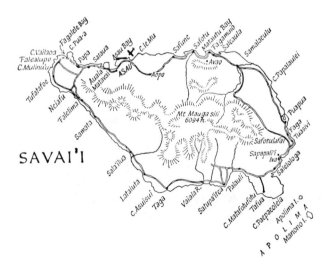

Many scholars believe what the Samoans have always believed – that Western Samoa is the cradle of Polynesia. Savai'i, the larger of the two main islands of Western Samoa, is identified as the legendary Hawaiki, the original home of the Polynesian people who were later to conquer the wide expanse of the blue Pacific in their waves of migrations north to Hawaii, east to Easter Island and south to New Zealand.

Beautiful beaches grace the Western Samoa shoreline. About a mile out to sea gray lines of reef encircle the land. The crashing waves are reduced by the reef into layers of white foam which disappear completely as they reach the peaceful lagoons.

Within the lagoons, that part of the sea between the beaches and the reef, the water is warm and calm. Inland, cool crystal clear fresh water abounds in the rivers, lakes and waterfalls. In the highlands lush mountains rise to great heights overlooking thousands of acres of tropical plantations, the shoreline and offshore islets.

UPOLU

FOR AGGIE

Foreword

This is not a travel story of the glamorous South Seas. Already there have been printed many hundreds of books extolling the virtues of the dusky island maidens, the tropical untouched paradises positively yearning for the inquisitive tourists, the leafy rain forests untouched by man. One could ramble on forever, but as the South Pacific travel folders emphasise, colourful island adventures are truly still there in abundance. Waiting to be discovered they are nowadays perhaps just a little further off the beaten tracks.

However this is definitely a story of the South Pacific, and in particular of Western Samoa. I have endeavoured to blend certain local history with the biography of a family which had its origin in Apia. It all began in 1891 when an English migrant chemist married a pretty Samoan village girl.

Today there are very many important and well known European names in the South Seas. Mostly planters or traders, they are families or clans descended from the pioneers of the early 1800s; settlers who came to the islands in the wake of the missionaries.

In Western Samoa there are many of these famous

families, now far extended, following mixed marriages with the Polynesians. The *aiga* or Samoan clan is a group entirely unknown in the European way of life. It can incorporate hundreds of relatives all of whom will gather together for weddings, funerals, and other festive occasions such as Christmas, birthdays, and inter-village cricket matches.

My story concerns a family such as this. Historically I think it is one of the most important clans in Samoa. This is a broad and debatable statement but I feel sure there are many who will agree with me.

The Swann family history is today a success story despite its ups and downs in the past. It now comprises an extended clan increased and widened like the present descendants of so many other groups of the pioneering European adventurers.

Aggie Grey is a Swann girl. Aggie is adamant that she is no more important than any other member of the Swann family. But one fact is undeniable — Aggie is known throughout the span of the Pacific, from Australasia to the USA.

Nowhere in the South Seas is there a hotelier as famed as Aggie. Since the end of World War II her name has been synonymous with Samoa. Aggie Grey's Hotel is today renowned for a friendly and homely atmosphere unique in the South Pacific.

Seldom ever is a living person other than royalty, portrayed on a postage stamp. This rare tribute was accorded Aggie in 1971 by the Samoan Government — a way to show their sincere appreciation of her tremendous contribution to the country's growing tourist industry.

This is a story of a charming and glamorous lady — Aggie Grey of Samoa — a legend in her lifetime.

N.E.

Chapter 1

Nineteenth-Century Migration

The picturesque Apia waterfront of today has changed very little since 1889 when an adventurous William J. Swann decided to try his luck at fame and fortune in the romantic islands of Samoa.

Certainly there are new buildings erected by the Germans, the New Zealanders, some by local traders, but Beach Road despite new twists and turns, still retains an old world atmosphere unmatched anywhere in the South Seas.

Swann was born in the English county of Lincolnshire on January 3, 1859, where his father James Butler Swann was a prosperous chemist. In the early 1860s, tempted by glowing reports of the riches to be won by hard-working pioneers in the far-flung colonies of the British Empire, the family of three boys and two girls migrated to New Zealand.

Those were the golden days so frequently recorded by historians emphasising the colossal spread of England's overseas possessions with that well-known phrase *the sun never sets on the British Empire*. And in those imperialistic days Britain certainly did rule the waves.

Nevertheless the venturesome pioneers were fully

aware of the trials and tribulations that awaited them especially in the more primitive of the under-developed Colonies. New Zealand was about as far removed east or west from their Lincolnshire home as the Swann family could expect to travel by ship — it was half way round the world.

By the time William was 17 he had completed his early education in New Zealand, so his father sent him to England to study chemistry.

Although an outstanding pupil in his class he was constantly tormented by acute homesickness. It was an ailment that served a good purpose for it urged him to complete his course so that he could be reunited with his family. William had no wish to stay in England indefinitely — his heart was firmly in the Antipodes, 15 000 miles away.

Restless in New Zealand, the Swann family decided to make another migratory move, this time a step deeper into the South Pacific. They arrived in Fiji on July 4, 1867, in the schooner *William and Mary*. It was in Levuka, then the administrative centre of the Fiji Islands, that James Butler Swann opened a chemist shop. He also experimented with cotton planting at Naikorokora on the banks of the Rewa River.

Fiji became a British colony on October 10, 1874 when Ratu Seru Cakobau ceded the islands to Queen Victoria. Levuka, on the island of Ovalau, remained the capital until 1882 when the administration transferred to Suva, some 80 miles away on Viti Levu.

William worked for quite a long time in the family shop. Those were honourable family days and a son would not think of leaving his father until his conscience cleared the indebtedness owed through his education.

In Levuka William earnestly studied medicine until he was thoroughly conversant with the best

14

treatment for many crippling tropical diseases of which little was known in England at that time. In this way the young chemist hoped his general knowledge might afford him an opportunity to explore more of the South Seas that he had grown to love so much.

He had already become a many-sided chemist— the type of versatile medical man irreplaceable even in the Pacific islands of today. It needs little imagination to realise just how valuable was the experience of such a trained professional one hundred years ago.

In the middle 1880s William was offered the prize post of ship's apothecary on the *Mohican*. She was a highly-respected American vessel that weaved a leisurely course through the islands dropping anchor at the more important trading ports of the South Seas.

His years aboard the *Mohican* afforded young Swann a wonderful opportunity to study the different peoples of the Pacific— the Melanesians, the Micronesians, and Polynesians. More than ever, he was interested in their cultures and varied customs especially the Fijians, the Tongans, and the Samoans. As ship's apothecary he acquired a unique proficiency in the handling of native people.

On their initial invasions medicine generally went hand in hand with the missionaries Bibles and the promotion of "Mother Hubbards", the neck-to-ankle garments for women. Probably their simply dispensed cure-all concoctions did more good to the suspicious recipients than did all the religious activities aimed at converting their pagan ways.

The problem for missionaries was to achieve even isolated native acceptance of European medicine. Deep-rooted customs were hard to change, for the Pacific islanders preferred their own native cures handed down through generations like their legends. Swann experienced the same difficulties, mastering these obstacles of opposition by exercising per-serverance and gentle persuasion with his patients.

Even today throughout the spread of the South Seas there are many native witch doctors who practise their cures for most of the indigenous complaints. Often a blind faith in the doctrine brings about a quicker recovery for the sick person than could ever be possible with European medicine.

It was the introduced diseases which had the witch doctors baffled. Unfortunately they often made face-saving attempts at a cure. Not until the very last, when all else had failed, would some sick persons hesitantly face up to attending a European medical centre.

Regrettably this situation still exists in many of the remote and even in some of the not-so-remote areas. Often the overdue journey to hospital is the last live one for the reluctant patient.

William, tiring of a life at sea, carefully searched the South Sea ports for an opportunity to continue his life as a chemist — somewhere to open a little dispensary far away from any strongly established opposition.

In Fiji, where William's two brothers were qualified chemists, the Swann family interests had expanded with the opening of a new pharmacy in Suva.

Then 30 years of age, William considered it was time to settle down. He had chosen Samoa but the final decision had not been easy. It had been necessary for William to temper his enthusiasm because he knew that it was innately polite for Samoans to agree with their superiors, particularly if they were *papalagi*.

Respect is a gravely important ingredient in

Polynesian culture. If *yes* is the answer that will gratify, then by all means say *yes* even if it means telling an outright lie.

It was obvious to the Samoans that this inquisitive *papalagi* asking so many questions about sicknesses and native medicines was anxious to settle in their country. Therefore they reasoned, irrespective of accuracy, to show their respect it must be *yes*, the answer that would please.

So although not lacking in optimism it must have been with a degree of inherent apprehension that ship's apothecary, William J. Swann, quit the sea forever and stepped ashore to begin a new life as a migrant chemist in Apia, Samoa.

Chapter 2
Apia 1889

In 1889 when Swann arrived in Samoa the country was seething like a volcano on the verge of eruption. Not only were the Samoans fighting among themselves, there was a continuous risk of open warfare between the three great powers, Germany, England, and the United States.

This was the sorry state of affairs after sixty years of European influence. Until Rev. John Williams, the pioneer missionary, landed in Savai'i in 1830 very little was known to the outside world of conditions in Western Samoa. Williams brought Christianity in his aptly named schooner, *Messenger of Peace*.

About 20 years later Apia began to take shape as the main port and commercial centre of Western Samoa.

The first trading firm of considerable standing was Johann Cesar Godeffroy and Sons, of Hamburg, who sent their representative from Valparaiso, Chile, in search of lucrative unknown outposts in the Pacific. He was August Unshelm, and his arrival in Apia in 1856, marked the real beginning of the German development in Western Samoa.

In the 1870s considerable rivalry began between

18

the world's three powerful nations — Great Britain, Germany and the United States, as to who was the ruling power in Samoa.

Meanwhile, the Samoans who had been fighting amongst themselves for over 20 years, were actually still independent. Certainly they were not particularly anxious to be "colonized" but they would have appreciated any foreign assistance that would have resulted in a peaceful independence. The Samoan fighting around Apia was intensifying to the worry of the European traders. Although great care was taken to see that no harm came to the 'foreigners', it was obviously becoming increasingly difficult to conduct trading posts under such appalling conditions.

At various times warships visited Samoa, endeavouring to bring about a peace. Great Britain and the United States were doing their utmost to this end, but Germany was gaining a solid foothold in the economy of the islands.

The consuls of the three nations became engaged in acts of intrigue that made Apia an early Lisbon or Casablanca of the Pacific. It was a game of chess, with three players, not one of whom was anxious to gamble on any risky moves.

During 1877 a party of Samoans visited the Fiji Islands asking for British protection but it was refused. In 1878 the group went to the United States again requesting protection, but returned with only the promise that a naval base would be established at Pago Pago.

Whilst the consuls were occupied in their diplomatic moves, the Samoan chiefs continued fighting for supremacy in and around Apia.

It became necessary for the British High Commissioner to proclaim the Municipality of Apia an international settlement somewhat like Shanghai.

Here European law was to be observed at all times, so that the chiefs had to confine their battles to other areas. The consuls of each of the three nations were members of the Apia Governing Board.

This was not the full answer to the problem. In fact it seemed that only a show of power was the alternative to the intrigue still being practised.

On Friday March 15, 1889, the most devastating hurricane in known history swept down on Samoa. It struck at a time when Apia harbour was filled with warships of the three nations — United States, Germany and Great Britain. There were seven altogether plus a large number of merchant ships.

There was a very good reason for this array of colors in Western Samoa at that particular time. Over the years Germany had doubtless established most of the trading that existed in the area, and now Berlin was of the opinion the islands should be annexed for the Fatherland.

This aim did not fit in with British and American thinking, and this resulted in tension running high, so much so that a conflict could have easily been the outcome.

Then Nature came to the rescue to thoroughly dampen the inflamed nationalism. In Apia the wind was coming from the south with accompanying heavy rain.

Next day there were definite signs of the weather worsening as the barometer continued to fall quite alarmingly.

Weather prophets ashore were adamant that this type of weather, coupled with the barometric conditions, was quite usual at the time of the year.

No one expected the hurricane which battered the fleet so severely that only the British *Calliope* escaped. Truly, it blew up a storm of peace.

The three American ships in the harbor were the *Trenton, Nipsic,* and *Vandalia.* From Germany were the *Adler, Eber,* and *Olga.*

Normally the gales blow into Apia from the northeast, but this time the winds struck dead from the north. The effect of this direction change meant that all the shipping was completely exposed to the fury of the most violent hurricane ever to strike Samoa.

The ships so haphazardly dragged their anchors throughout the night that by morning the entire fleet was much closer inshore. At five o'clock in the afternoon the *Eber* was thrown onto the reef, where she appeared to break up.

The *Vandalia,* dragging its anchor, was gradually bearing down on the *Trenton* which had aboard the Commander-in-Chief of the Pacific Station, Rear Admiral L.A. Kimberley.

Next morning at 7.30 the *Nipsic,* which was one of the innermost ships, was blown ashore onto a bank of sand. Five of the crew lost their lives while struggling to reach safety.

Germany's *Adler* was in considerable danger when at 8 a.m. she grazed the reef with her stern. The sea was running with frightening force, so violently that the *Adler* was lifted bodily out of the water, and deposited on top of the reef.

The crew lived on board for about 24 hours, experiencing a very severe buffeting from the seas breaking over the reef. Fortunately all hands were rescued, but the total of wrecked ships was now three; *Nipsic, Eber,* and *Adler.*

The four still afloat had plenty to worry about as the *Vandalia* continued to drag its anchors and bore down on the *Trenton,* riding perilously close to a reef.

Meanwhile the *Olga* was having extreme difficulty in not crashing into the *Calliope,* but the British ship with its powerful engines managed to keep at least six feet away from the reef.

Eventually Captain Kane commanding the *Calliope* was faced with a decision to make a run for the open sea, risking the ship and the crew, or beach the vessel. Beaching would possibly wreck the ship but would save the lives of the crew.

In "Samoan Hurricane," a Naval Historian Foundation publication, the skipper relates that he decided to head for the open sea . . . 'accordingly I slipped the cables and went hard ahead calling up every pound of steam, every revolution of the screw.

'In fact, everything was working as hard as it could go. In making the passage, the vessel literally stood on end — the water coming in at the bows as she dipped, running off aft immediately she arose.'

He continues: 'I managed to clear the *Vandalia* without mishap, but went so close to the *Trenton* as to put her fore yard-arm over her deck. As the *Calliope* lifted up she rolled to port and the fore yard over the *Trenton* just cleared her.'

The flagship *Trenton* was now helpless but her crew lined the deck when the *Calliope* made its dash, and as one man they gave the British vessel three ringing cheers to help it on its way.

This was one of the many touching scenes of the hurricane, Capt. Kane saying it brought tears to their eyes, so wonderful did they consider the Americans' gesture.

The *Calliope* managed to clear the reef by a narrow margin, but although being driven at top speed she travelled barely a half-mile in one hour. Nevertheless, she had managed to escape by literally running the gauntlet.

The *Vandalia* was sinking quickly, forcing her crew to climb the rigging and the masts. Many were rescued by the *Trenton* on which they remained until the winds subsided.

The *Olga* and the *Trenton* were further damaged during a collision, but without loss of life.

After the storm a roll call revealed the death toll:- *Vandalia* — 43; *Nipsic* — 7; *Eber* — 76; *Adler* — 20; and the *Trenton* — 1. In addition large numbers of injured were treated by missionaries or the Samoans.

Even when the hurricane was at its worst, there were hundreds of Samoans under the leadership of Seumanutafa, chief of Apia village, assisting the sailors to safety.

In the emergency that existed, the Samoans gave no partisan thought to whether the "foreigners" were Americans, British, or Germans. They risked their own lives to save those unfortunates struggling to reach the shore.

Before dawn on Sunday the 17th the gale had moderated and the seas were falling.

To show its appreciation of the courageous rescue work the United States Government generously bestowed gifts on the villagers. The Germans showed their appreciation with a payment of three dollars for each of their men saved.

This calamity seems to have been the main reason why the three powers gathered around the conference table to sign the 1889 Berlin Treaty. The agreement called for an independent Samoa ruled by King Malietoa Laupepa, with the Apia Governing Board still in authority in the township area.

The peace did not last very long. Rival factions challenged the position of Malietoa, so much so that fighting again erupted throughout Samoa.

Swann went about setting up his first chemist shop in Apia undaunted by the actions of the three interloping great powers who were continually plotting and planning their island strategies. His store occupied a prominent position in Beach Road near the present offices of Polynesian Airlines.

Just about this time the famous writer and poet, Robert Louis Stevenson was sailing the schooner *Equator* through the South Seas, forever in search of a climate kindly to his tubercular condition. With him were his mother, his wife Fanny and stepson Lloyd.

In December, 1889, the Stevenson family first landed in Apia, Western Samoa, where they rented a small house. Louis loved the country and bought land which eventually became the estate of Vailima. In a letter to Charles Baxter in February, 1890, Stevenson wrote: "I bought 314½ acres of beautiful land in the bush behind Apia. We will get the house built, the garden laid . . . I have paid one-half of it. Should I fail to meet the next payment H.J. Moors of Apia will draw on you personally for the amount of US$10 currency to the acre — at $7 to the £, 157¼ acres, it makes about £200."

Harry Jay Moors was an American trader, one of the ablest, wealthiest and best informed of the non-German merchants in Apia.

Louis quickly had the jungle cleared so that a temporary home could be constructed.

Soon on the move again, the Stevenson family boarded the *Lubeck* in Apia Harbor during February, 1890, bound for Sydney. This was to be the first stage of the voyage as Fanny and Louis were anxious to go on to England.

But fate was to intervene when Louis became seriously ill in Sydney. At first it was thought that a sea trip to England would help the patient, but thinking deeper into the problem they realised that it was only sea travel in the South Seas that rallied

Louis. So Fanny got her husband to sea, this time to cruise for over three months in the *Janet Nichol* amongst the islands he was yearning to know.

On May 1, 1890, when they again called at Apia, Louis was apparently in excellent health. Unfortunately the progress was shortlived as he suddenly became ill on their return to Sydney.

By this time the family was convinced it was the climate of Samoa that constituted the prescription for good health that Louis needed most. Back to Apia they came in the *Lubeck* arriving in September 1890 to take up residence in what was the beginning of Vailima.

Because Stevenson was always anxious to hear of any new drug discoveries that might alleviate his condition, he became a frequent visitor to the Swann pharmacy. Before long a close friendship developed between the writer and the chemist. Swann frequently visited Vailima and treated the Stevenson family for prevailing tropical complaints ranging from prickly heat and "Samoan tummy" to bouts of influenza and pneumonia.

Swann was now firmly established in Apia — he had found his niche in the South Seas, his business was flourishing. Time then to look for a wife, and once more his shrewd approach to the age-old gamble was rewarded by a friendship with the beautiful and gentle Pele of Toamua village.

Some years ago a grand old lady of Toamua, Puapa'e, told me of the romance.

"Our village was very proud," she recalled, "when it was obvious there was to be a wedding between one of our girls and such an important *papalagi*.

"In those days Pele was quite young to be a bride, but they were very much in love. She was about twenty, very religious, and attended the Catholic

25

Mission School at Savalalo near the present Grand Theatre."

The father of Pele was Maiava of Toamua village and her mother was Simativa, a daughter of Seumanutafa, a high chief of Apia village. She had a brother Misi and a sister Pala.

In 1891 Swann and Pele were married at Safune, Toamua, with a Roman Catholic service conducted by a European priest. The chiefs and orators of the village considered the wedding to be of the greatest importance so it was celebrated with speeches, *kava*, feasting, and dancing of the highest order.

"I was only a youngster at the time," reminisced Puapa'e, "but I have never forgotten the way we Samoans sang and danced after their marriage."

That night in Toamua village by the light of a flickering oil lamp I talked for hours with Puapa'e for she was one of the very few still living who could remember the time when Swann came to the shores of her country.

The old lady had these vivid memories of the past so firmly entrenched in her mind that she could recall them with no apparent difficulty. In minute detail she talked of those events of eighty years ago just as though they had happened only yesterday.

As might be expected, an honoured guest at the wedding was the bridegroom's close friend Robert Louis Stevenson. *Tusitala* loved an opportunity to enjoy himself at any *fiafia*, especially those which were far removed from any stuffy government involvement.

Although he detested the consuls for the intrigues they were practising Stevenson did attend many official functions in Apia's "decrepit" Town Hall, where, in his words, he "danced the quadrille, rackety and prancing and embraceatory beyond words."

26

It was during these troubled in-between times while the great powers schemed and when Samoa's independence hung by a thread, that the Lincolnshire chemist, William Swann, brought his wife, Pele, from Toamua village to live with him above his pharmacy in Beach Road.

I talked with Mrs. Rosa Papali'i Ryan, an elderly lady who had wonderful stories to unfold of the past. She clearly remembered Pele and many happenings before the turn of the century in Apia.

"Happily married to Pele, Swann was in the envious position of having many servants," Rosa said.

"Although they were *aiga* from Toamua he generously paid the help," she recalled. "Pele was highly regarded, especially known for her gentle nature. Not only was she well versed in Samoan affairs, but as Mrs. Swann she was greatly respected for her wide knowledge of European customs."

Swann had married in 1891, and like most other European traders, was to waste little time in beginning a family. There was great rejoicing on July 29, 1893 when a daughter, Margaret Pele, was born at their home above the chemist's shop in Beach Road.

Maggie Swann was a little over four years of age when Aggie (Agnes Genevieve) was born on 31 October, 1897.

The third Swann girl, Violet Mary, was born on 31 August, 1899. These three girls, Maggie, Aggie and Mary were destined to become famous as the "Swann bouquet" — the toast of Apia town.

27

Chapter 3

R. L. Stevenson's Days in Apia

So many stories have been written about Robert Louis Stevenson's short life in Samoa that it would be unnecessarily repetitive to discuss it at length in this book.

However it is his association with Swann that is an important segment of this particular history. Stevenson ever encouraged the migrant chemist, for Swann had many problems even after he was firmly established as a trader.

These were not only the usual Pacific island shipping arrival uncertainties effecting supplies, but national jealousies and intrigues which extended beyond the political levels into the business world.

One instance occurred shortly after the Germans assumed control, when G. Sabiel, an envious opposition chemist, proposed to run Swann out of Apia. Established in business near the present Land and Survey Department in Beach Road, Sabiel approached the Customs Department for special privileges as a German national.

R. P. Berking, the Collector of Customs from 1905 until 1914 told me that he would not agree to Sabiel's proposals. He ruled that Swann already had his business established in Samoa "where everyone had the same rights."

Berking, an early settler in Samoa, was one of Apia's best known and respected citizens. However, it was really only by accident that he came to the islands.

Born in 1880 in Hanover, where his father was an innkeeper, young Berking, when seventeen, left home to rove the world. From America he went to Hawaii where he stopped for three years working on a sugar plantation.

In Hawaii he received his call-up for German military service. The most convenient German possession at which he could report was Samoa, so in 1900 he went to Apia. After a medical check-up Berking was classed as unfit because of short sight. He settled in Samoa, enjoyed a chequered life interspersed with visits back to Germany, and was 92 when he died in Apia in 1972.

During Stevenson's time most Europeans enjoyed an occasional meal in town although good restaurants were practically non-existent. *Tusitala*, "writer" in Samoan, always had his dining-out "tiffin" at a shanty run by a Chinese named Kai Sue. The dining room extended to the waters edge where the waves gently lapped at the feet of the diners.

Kai Sue and his wife Ula who gave special preference to Stevenson, would waste little time in bundling outside any Samoans who happened to be occupying his regular table.

Tusitala and Swann always enjoyed talking with the Chinaman who never failed to reminisce of his enforced experiences as a cook for Bully Hayes, one of the best-known blackbirders of the South Seas. After he had been shanghaied aboard Bully's schooner, Kai became the pirate's cook for over two years.

It seemed that Bully Hayes was quite a connoisseur of food, and Kai Sue excelled in producing the specialities of his past master for customers of their Apia restaurant.

Once Stevenson asked the Chinaman why he stayed with Hayes.

"Oh, me made stay," replied Kai Sue, "but vely bad fo' me, me no likey schooner. Me Chinaman and gentleman, Bully Hayes damn pirate!"

Stevenson and Swann appreciated a quiet beer at the restaurant, but whenever ladies were in the dinner party, *Tusitala* usually arranged for bottles of his favourite dry champagne from Vailima to be cooled down in readiness for the evening.

Maggie, Swann's eldest daughter, can boast of being alive during Stevenson's time in Samoa, but she is not able to say she knew the famous *Tusitala* for the storyteller's chequered life was soon to be ended.

Late in the afternoon of December 3, 1894, Stevenson clasped his head with his long bony hands exclaiming "What a terrible pain!" His wife Fanny helped him to a couch in the great hall of Vailima where he quickly lapsed into unconsciousness.

While he appeared to be sleeping soundly, Fanny felt his pulse slowly ebbing and at a little after eight o'clock Robert Louis Stevenson died.

The sad news quickly spread through the town of Apia and the entire island. Of his good friends one of the first to arrive was High Chief Tuimaleali'ifana, who seated cross-legged beside the body of R.L.S. emotionally — and as only a trained orator is capable — voiced the lament of all Samoans. *"Tatou moni Tusitala. Ua tagi le fatu ma le eleele."* ("Our beloved *Tusitala*. The stones and the earth weep.")

Stevenson's sudden death was a great blow to Swann. Over the years they had become such close friends that the chemist felt a sincere personal loss.

Aggie Grey told me her father often talked about the burial of *Tusitala*. So impressive and solemn was the funeral that she clearly remembered her father's detailed stories.

Aggie explained that it had been always understood that Stevenson wished to be buried on the summit of Mt. Vaea which was part of the Vailima estate. The mountain is about 1,200 feet above sea level and some 600 feet from the base to the peak.

In those times in the tropical climate of Samoa it would be necessary to bury R.L.S. the next day. Therefore to honor his wish it was imperative for an urgent plan of action to be systematically carried out during the remainder of the night.

In October, 1894, there had been a touching presentation to Stevenson of *Alo Loto Alofa* ("The Road of the Loving Heart"), a new road from Apia to Vailima. The whole construction cost was borne by the Mata'afa chiefs. The gesture was in gratitude to Stevenson for all he had done for them — "It shall never be muddy; it shall endure for ever, this road that we have dug."

Walking up the "Road of the Loving Heart" to the gateway of the residence a gathering of Samoan chiefs discussed a plan which called for each of their men to be allotted a length of the mountainside of Mt. Vaea which he would clear of growth so that a pathway could be formed for the funeral procession.

There were 200 volunteers with swinging axes and bush knives working only by the light of the stars. The darkness seemed to have little effect on the precision of the Samoans in carrying out this task.

Perhaps the thought was that this was one way to pay homage to their beloved *Tusitala*. It was certainly no mean feat to clear the track felling trees up to 50 feet in height with a diameter of two feet and more.

Rolling clouds of mist across the mountain tops heralded the break of dawn, but the Samoans did not rest.

As each finished his allotted length of track, he either went to the summit to assist in the digging of a shallow grave or else to the beach to bring back coral pebbles and crushed lava-rock to provide the *fanua loto* or bed on which the body would rest.

This rock treatment is normally reserved for royal burials, the body being wrapped in many layers of rugs and *siapo* (tapa). Stevenson however, had the traditional European-type coffin constructed by the local carpenter.

The body was prepared for burial by rubbing it with coconut oil scented with the fragrance of the flowers of the moso'oi tree. *(Canangium odoratum).*

He was dressed as the Samoans knew him, wearing his well-known velvet jacket. Over his frail body was spread the Union Jack.

As he lay at rest in the Vailima hall, the arrival of chiefs was marked by the giving of fine mats, the greatest tribute they could possibly make to the memory of their *Tusitala*.

When it was time for the funeral party to leave, a high chief of considerable standing led the way, followed by a mourner who at intervals blew low notes on a conch shell.

Fanny had been advised not to attempt the long climb to the summit, so three members of the family represented her at the burial.

The Reverend Mr. Clarke, who had been the first person to greet R.L.S. in Samoa, walked slowly behind the four chiefs bearing the coffin, down a quarter-mile gentle slope to the foot of Mt. Vaea.

Groups of four men had been stationed at various

intervals along the steep climb to the summit. The coffin was passed carefully from group to group until it finally reached the peak.

At the Presbyterian burial service, Mr. Clarke paid homage to his friend. Then followed speeches from Samoans using the eloquence of oratory for which they are renowned.

At the end of the prayers, four Samoans stepped into the wide and shallow grave to receive the coffin. Gently it was laid to rest on the base of the coral pebbles and lava-rock. After the earth was filled in and a mound formed, the grave was lined with black stones, which also indicate royalty.

Fanny remained in Apia for several years and before she left she commissioned Gelett Burgess to erect a tomb that would serve as a fitting memorial to her husband. Rather than lean to any ornamentation, Burgess constructed a plain tomb consisting of blocks of finely-mixed cement. The tomb with its bronze plaques, is preserved to this day on the peak of Mt. Vaea.

Apia village was the home of Aggie's grandmother, Simativa, daughter of the chief Seumanutafa. In the earliest days it is possible that the sprawl of the villages extended to where Aggie Grey's Hotel is now located.

Throughout the South Seas the more select locations were to be found around the coasts. Not far inland were volcanic mountains as rugged as anywhere in the world, mostly overgrown with creeper-tangled rain forests through which the sun seldom penetrated.

History concerning the origins of village names is not so jealously guarded. The chiefs feel that these particular traditions belong to the *aigi* to discuss if they wish.

There are conflicting tales to be heard about the beginnings of almost every village. The origin of Apia and how it got its name, is not known by many Samoans. If you ask around you may hear two different stories but these will come from very few people.

One legend tells that before the Europeans came, the Samoans mostly lived a short distance inland from the sea, whereas today there are mainly only coastal villages. Regularly the people came to the coast to fish and to procure seawater for cooking purposes. A chief from Solosolo with his fishing party discovered Apia Harbour had plenty of fish so they built several *fales* on the shore and stayed there for a longer time than usual.

A group of girls from an inland village on a *malaga* to the coast to collect seawater discovered the new settlement and the fishermen.

They hurried back to their village and reported to the chief that the bay was inhabited. *Apia*, which is used in many Polynesian dialects, means habitation or home. In Samoan it may be translated as temporary abode.

W. von Bulow, in Die Geschichte de Stammvaters der Samoaner (Berlin 1898) contends that Apia got its name from *apilitia* or *apitia*, words that were used to describe the fate of the Manono people in a tribal war on Upolu.

Many warriors from Manono who were killed were buried where the original iceworks used to stand. Now the area is called Tanugamanono, the burial place of the Manono people.

Apilitia which may be shortened to *apitia*, means hemmed in or surrounded and von Bulow thinks it was further abbreviated to *apia*.

In 1861 Theodor Weber, like August Unshelm, came to Samoa through the Valparaiso branch of the mighty Hamburg house, Johann Cesar Godeffroy and Sons. His first advice to European immigrants was "to secure a woman of your own, no matter what island you take her from, because a trader without a wife is forever in hot water."

Weber's suggestions which were good counselling in those pioneer days, continue to be followed even now in the 1970s. Admittedly there are certainly more matrimonial problems involved these days, but many lonely Europeans living in the South Seas do just what Weber recommended in 1861.

First the missionaries in Samoa and then the traders acquired the choicest lands from the chiefs in exchange for trifles such as rusty nails or a few bowls of colourful baubles.

In addition to his advice to acquire a wife, pioneer Theodor Weber emphasised to newly-arrived traders that they should "give no assistance to missionaries either by word or deed beyond what is demanded of you by common humanity. Although the missionaries bought the choicest land with trinkets they now tell the natives that cloth and coin are better payment for produce than beads and tobacco."

Samoa had no written language before the coming of the European, and the genealogy of the tribe or clan is methodically passed down through the ages from father to his immediate successor. Not only has this all-important descent of ancestors been relayed from the bygone eras but so have the countless tales, legends and myths.

Always a formidable obstacle to the assembling of authentic information regarding culture and folklore is the inherent reluctance of the Samoan to divulge these traditions to other than his heir. To the Samoan this knowledge is strictly a personal matter, so profoundly secret that its publication would deprive the family of an untold amount of prestige and honour.

A chief known to possess a wealth of traditional knowledge is held in the highest esteem. This dignified position as a sage he endeavours to preserve for himself during his lifetime so that when the time arrives he may pass it intact to his successor.

In an address to the Samoan Research Society in 1923, O.F. Nelson, son of August Nelson who migrated to Samoa in 1868, began by saying that "When I first became interested in Samoan legends and folklore some 23 years ago (1900) I trusted too much to memory and made notes only of odd names and places."

Nelson regretted that "most of my notes have been mislaid, but even now when I hear these matters discussed I am generally able to recall what I had written about them in the past. It is quite possible for a Samoan chief whose principal duty is to keep the legends ever in mind, to hold a fairly authentic record, so that most of the traditions now held are as reliable as can be expected under such a system."

*　　*　　*

On one occasion when Stevenson was writing critically of the political situation in Western Samoa he likened it to a horse race, with Germany, the United States and Great Britain jockeying for positions.

This international intrigue continued in Samoa until near the turn of the century when there was a sudden finish to the drama of the past decade.

The year 1899 found Great Britain engaged in the Boer War campaign in South Africa. The British were faring so badly that they were in no position to argue when Germany insisted that the 1889 Berlin Treaty be scrapped.

Under a new treaty Germany was given the rights to annex Western Samoa and the United States permitted to control Eastern Samoa as a territory under the administration of the U.S. Navy Department, whilst Britain agreed that it would forego all claims to Western Samoa.

So began a great period of advance in Western Samoa with roads and buildings being constructed everywhere to meet the demands of the growing trade.

The German Empire was to make itself felt throughout the Pacific and one of its most important outposts was Apia, Samoa.

Chapter 4
The German Era (1899-1914)

The first news of the partition of Samoa, or the outcome of the Convention as it was officially called, reached Apia from Europe late in November, 1899. In those days there was no cable or radio communication and the majority of news came by ship from New Zealand.

In this case it was the s.s. *Manapouri* that brought the cable of glad tidings to Dr. Wilhelm Solf then holding the position of President of the Municipality of Apia. The receipt and despatch of most cables were channeled through New Zealand where there was a connection with Europe.

New Zealand has always had a keen interest in the destiny of Samoa. A mistaken conclusion exists that the Dominion was unconcerned for Samoa until ordered to occupy the islands at the outbreak of World War I in 1914.

On three occasions before the 1899 Convention, New Zealand had unsuccessfully urged Great Britain to take possession of Samoa. In 1894 they went so far as to offer to administer the islands if they became a British protectorate like Tonga, or alternatively to assume control on behalf of the Treaty Powers.

New Zealand went a step further and offered to send an occupation force of 500 troops equipped with machine guns. The British Government rejected the proposal but instead commissioned a Dominion ship as a courier to take secret despatches to Samoa.

Dr. Solf received an official communique from Germany in February, 1900, appointing him as the first Governor. Of paramount importance were instructions for the earliest possible implementation of a ceremony to take possession of Western Samoa for the Fatherland.

On March 1 at Mulinu'u Point, a peninsula steeped in history as the burial place of kings and high chiefs, Dr. Solf hoisted the German flag. The European population was there in force. They were not disappointed with the show, a brass band from the *Cormoran*, a warship anchored in the harbour, played stirring martial tunes to the gathering.

Dr. Solf proclaimed the annexation for the Kaiser saying, "We hereby in the name of the German Empire take these islands under our Imperial protection."

Then began a period of progress and great advancement in Western Samoa, probably the greatest step forward ever in the country's history. Life for the European rulers was not without its problems, however, for very soon groups of Samoan chiefs showed their resentment to the strict German rule.

The German administration never did have much time for the infiltrating island missionaries. Whenever possible they would subject them to direct or subtle ridicule. It was in December, 1903 that the Wright Brothers flew their biplane at Kitty Hawk, USA. Even before that first aeroplane flight the somewhat vulgar reference to a preacher as a "sky pilot" was already in common use in Samoa. A report from the

Samoanische Zeitung of May 30, 1903 tells that, "the custom of a lot of gay young school girls spending their holidays away from home at the house of the village parson, is as a rule, a fairly good business for the dusky sky pilot, as numbers of young men visit them at night. Each one brings a present of a tin of salmon, meat, biscuits, bread or something similar. If the girls are clever enough to get two crowds running in opposition to each other the wily parson is apt to reap a rich harvest of foodstuffs."

During the early days of the occupation the Swann family business prospered as more traders brought about a controlled economy previously unknown in Samoa.

As an island group Samoa is prone to earthquake and volcanic activity. Although frequent minor shakes are continuously recorded, there has been nothing in known history as violent as the Savai'i eruptions that began in October, 1902.

The lava initially flowed quickly and subsided quickly with little further activity until mid-August 1905. At the time Aggie was eight so she was able to recall much of the excitement in Apia as news reached her father of fresh outbreaks on Savai'i.

The first signs of trouble were some slight quake shocks felt in Apia. Aggie's father told her that Captain Reid of the cutter *Ethel* first reported a colossal activity renewal that he saw when anchored off the north coast.

Villagers exitedly described how ashes and smoke were belching from the mountain followed by molten lava pouring down the sides of the volcano. The eruptions were about eight miles east of the 1902 explosive points. When lava reached the Safatu plantations the understandably worried Samoans held daily meetings in the villages.

As stories reached Apia of the volcano's activity, then intensified to some twenty earth-shuddering quakes each day, the locals began to have some fears that Upolo might be destined for the same fate as Savai'i. There was nothing Governor Solf could do to dispel these rumours nor could he convince the superstitious Samoans that German rule was not to blame for the whole catastrophe.

Aggie told of the many expeditions that set out from Apia to visit the Savai'i volcano. After reaching Safune by boat the parties would ride horses for about 1½ hours into the interior to a plantation which was within reasonable walking distance of the craters. At one time the surface area of the boiling lava was said to extend over 25 acres.

The lava had a twelve-mile passage to the sea where spectacular jets of steam rocketed high into the air. It was not until late in 1911 that the eruption quietened and the lava ceased flowing.

Over the years much rich land had been devastated as can be seen on a map of Savai'i. Nowadays vegetation is gradually returning, led by the "mile-a-minute" creeper, but the land has been lost to cultivation for a long time.

For tourists driving over the moon-like surface of the Savai'i lava field there is one particular miracle they should study. It is the Virgin's Grave where a Samoan Roman Catholic novice from the convent in Lealatele was buried.

Her grave had been covered with the usual concrete slab and raised a couple of feet.

Heading for the sea the molten lava bore down on the little church, bringing down the roof as it rolled onward and smothering everything in its path. In this locality the lava averages a depth of six feet and must have had unrelenting power.

Yet when the lava reached the grave of the novice the flow separated and reunited after it had passed the burial place of the girl.

To this day one can gaze six feet down through the solidified black lava and clearly see, as if at the bottom of a well, the miracle of the Virgin's Grave, completely untouched by the molten mass of the eruptions.

*   *   *

In January, 1903 Pele died at the age of 31 and was buried at the Marist Brothers cemetery at Savalolo. It was a sad time for Swann, now the father of four children, Maggie, Aggie, Mary, and baby Willie. With his growing business he did not have much free time. Not only was Swann a pharmacist, he was a doctor to the Samoans as well as being a capable dentist able to extract teeth with considerable skill.

The schooldays of the Swann girls during the German occupation were very happy times. There were always exciting parties for the children of the European community and Aggie well remembers the way these and the grander adult functions were arranged. Everyone wore their best regalia, there were wonderful things to feast upon, as the Germans tried their hardest to win over the population.

Some of the parties catered for hundreds of guests for these were the glorious days of the colonial rule of the mighty Fatherland. There were circular European bandstands built for the brass bands and whenever a warship visited Apia, Beach Road vibrated with martial music. There was a bandstand in the town centre near where the clock tower, a World War I memorial, was later built. The construction of bandstands was but an insignificant facet of the building programme.

A bonanza of houses, godowns, and office buildings appeared in the comparatively short span of the German occupation.

A big percentage of the buildings of that era has lasted for more than seventy years, in fact many of them are in constant use today. The Government offices and Supreme Court continue to be dominant in the tropical white wooden architecture of Beach Road. Just as the German masters gazed out of their verandah-shaded windows across the entrance to Apia Harbour to the broad expanses of the Pacific Ocean, so today do the administrators of a proud independent Western Samoa.

*   *   *

It should not be assumed that the German rule was a period of complete peace, progress, and tranquility in Samoa. Many and varied were the problems as Aggie remembered. The Germans were well aware that the Samoans were not good plantation workers so they lost little time in bringing in Chinese coolies to carry the brunt of the labor force.

The first of the bonded immigrants from China reached Apia in April, 1903, a batch of 276. Before the end of 1909 there were over 1,000 of the contract laborers in Samoa. When the s.s. *Mathilde* arrived in November, 1909, it brought another 600 and few returned home to the Orient. The coolie problem seemed solved for the Germans, who gladly acquiesced to a request for the establishment in Apia of a Chinese consul to hear any complaints.

There were plenty of instances of brutality on both sides, even murder. The Germans were paying for slave labor and there are always some slaves who will rebel against such authority.

Treatment of protesting Samoans had to be regarded differently, even in the colonial days of the early 1900s. As Governor Solf said, "While not losing sight of the natural desire of our Government to have some advantage from its colonies, never forget that they are the homelands of human people who have been promised our protection, and for whom we must provide."

The Germans did rule very firmly, too firmly for many Samoans who began to regret their loss of independence. Gradually the power and influence of the chiefs were being diminished in various ways and with an ever-increasing regularity.

During the absence of Dr. Solf in 1905, selected high chiefs sent a petition to the Kaiser, unbeknown to the Acting-Governor, Dr. Schultz. The Samoans requested the return of their authority and more privileges from the Government. They considered they should have the right of operating co-operative trading ventures — that all trade should not remain a monopoly of the Germans.

Unrealistic decisions on this request were the forerunner of the greatest troubles that beset the Germans during their occupation. Governor Solf returned to Apia aboard a warship and quickly assessed the situation. However his strong action in dismissing all of the Samoan advisers, even those he had himself appointed, was not the solution. It was this action that sowed the seed to the underground movement, the *Mau*, a group that in most countries would forever be called the "freedom fighters."

When Dr. Solf assumed Governorship in 1900 he said that most decisions even the most important would be made by his authority. Berlin was far away and direct cables still non-existent in 1905. There were several well-known easy ways to be rid of troublemakers — send them to gaol or deportation to Saipan, part of a German colony in the Marianas. The 1905 troubles were accounted for, at least temporarily, by these means.

Discontent continued amongst the Samoans until in 1908 even European and part-Samoan traders were expressing their dissatisfaction with conditions. They had not as yet openly linked forces against the Germans but an underground collaboration was evident.

Early in 1909 there was a confrontation with the Germans as the *Mau* movement came to the surface. At this stage the rebels had more or less become a militant body with their most powerful armament being the shotguns generously licenced by the Germans for the purpose of shooting pigeons.

The *Mau* leader, a chief named Lauati from Savai'i, allegedly told the Germans he was carrying out the wishes of the paramount chiefs. This may have been the case, but the root of the trouble was the dissatisfaction brought about by so much loss of Samoan authority under the German rule.

Complaints, many and varied, were mostly treated with complacency by the administrators. Poll tax, or head tax, as it was unofficially called, was introduced as a revenue earner. The Samoans unsuccessfully protested that it reduced them to the status of animals. In 1903 the tax had been amended so that a *matai* paid twelve marks a year and a non-titled Samoan only four marks.

The Germans realised there would be some identification problems in the new ruling and emphasised that "it may be rather difficult for whites to distinguish between a *matai* and a *taulealea* (untitled) but there would be no doubts amongst the Samoans in this respect." The *Samoanische Zeitung* went on to say that "in the case of such doubt the *pulenuu* decision is final."

Lauati and his *Mau* followers had fomented the most serious rebellion since German rule began. A greatly worried Governor Solf sent an urgent message calling for help to Fiji for relay by cable to the Kaiser.

Usually in good control of his colony the Governor panicked and exaggerated the real situation. Oldtime German residents say the problem could have been resolved by a combination of *fa'a-Samoa* talks and the usual Solf diplomacy. However, it was not to be and the Kaiser viewed the uprising with considerable concern.

Aggie, who was only twelve at the time, remembered the troubles. Although too young to understand the real causes, her father later clearly explained the underlying problems that brought about the display of force by the Fatherland.

"In March, 1909," Aggie said, "the German Asiatic Naval Squadron hurriedly sailed from China to uplift Solomon Island troops from the New Guinea colony. Although Solf had a sizable contingent of Samoan police at his disposal he was loathe to use them against their own people. He knew, however, that a show of more than two hundred black soldiers would make a very effective impression on the rebels.

"The 1909 *Mau* leaders were mainly from Savai'i villages where there was a British resident-representative, Richard Williams. Solf sent a message through Williams for Lauati and his followers to come to Apia for peace talks but there was no response from the protestors.

"Meanwhile the Solomon Islanders who were housed in the Ififi school, were becoming impatient for some sort of action. Finally Solf gave Lauati three days to appear in Apia otherwise he would order the soldiers to Savai'i with instructions to burn their villages.

"The *Mau* leaders rejected the ultimatum and without delay the Governor despatched his soldiers to Savai'i.

"As can be imagined," Aggie continued, "the sight of the armed black troops was too much for the Samoans. They surrendered, begging that their villages be spared, and Solf agreed."

The 1909 bloodless revolution had come to an end. There were arrests but no trials. In April Lauati together with seventy chiefs, their wives, children, and an LMS pastor, went aboard the warships bound for unlimited exile on Saipan.

But the *Mau* had not been completely quashed. It went underground and lived to fight another day.

At this time the International Hotel right opposite the Swann pharmacy was advertising saltwater bathing and freshwater showers — billiards and bagatelle, commodious sample room for travellers. The Apia Sports Club always had several race meetings each year; without fail on the Kaiser's birthday, October 22. Aggie thought that the Germans gave tourism considerable assistance and organised novelty trips whenever possible.

For the local people there were regular weekend visits to the active Savai'i volcano. Although news from overseas was always late in reaching Samoa there was a very well patronised free reading room at the Central Hotel. Under flapping punkah fans most well-known German magazines and newspapers were in continual demand by the European community. For those who had a yearning for a bush weekend the Germans installed cooking utensils and other camping equipment at the beautiful Lake Lanuto'o situated inland some ten miles from Apia.

From 1909 until 1914 the years in German Samoa passed quietly for the Swann family. Maggie, Aggie and Mary enjoyed the gay times, the concerts, the innumerable tea parties that had become their way of life.

New roads and buildings continued to be constructed so that soon it was not necessary for families journeying from village to village to go by canoe. They could walk around the coastline on well built roads carrying their baskets of *taro*, coconuts and bananas.

The big German trading firm Deutschen Handels und Plantagen Gessellschaft (DH & PG) built the rambling Casino on the beach front as a residential for their staff. In the decades that followed the solidly-built tropical guest house was a byword in Samoa, surpassed only in later years by Aggie's Hotel.

In the first decade of German rule the European community had shown very little aggression to the colonial administration — it had been the Samoans who were in a perpetual state of simmering rebellion. Then in 1910 a group of five Europeans led by O. F. Nelson sent a strongly-worded petition to Berlin setting out their complaints of excessive taxation.

They emphasised that the administration and the laws were biased against the non-German community. The petition stressed full agreement with the native Samoans' dissatisfaction of their limited representation in the running of the colony. O. F. Nelson was to become a leader of the *Mau* movement in the years that followed — a true freedom fighter and a martyr in the cause of Western Samoa Independence.

★   ★   ★

Maggie, a good scholar, had regular music lessons

Aggie, age 16

Aggie's mother, Pele, 1900

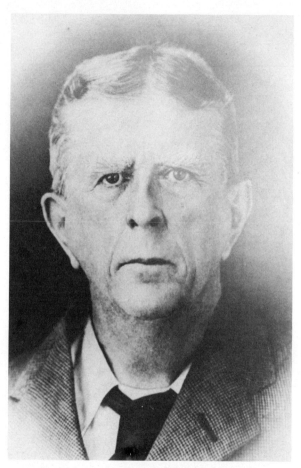

Aggie's father, William J. Swann

Aggie,   Mary

During World War I

Maggie   Mary, Frederick and Daisy

Apia Harbour, 1899

Ornate Certificate awarded to William J. Swann, 1919

A. J. Tattersall, 1906

Robert ("Obliging Bob")
Easthope, 1906

August Nelson, 1906

R. L. Stevenson

August Nelson's store, 1906

Casino Hotel, 1960

Aggie with granddaughter Aggie, 1979

Aggie and Charles G

Anna Stancil, 1979

Aggie and grandson Frederick

William Willis and Alan Grey, 1964

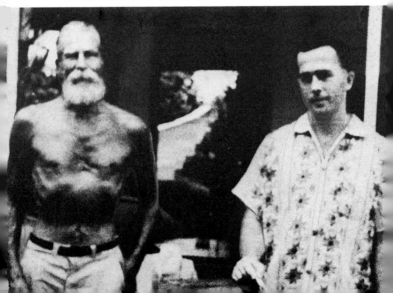

Aggie and the author, 1979

A Samoan village *fale*

Apia Protestant Church —
Aggie was married here

Birthplace of the Swann girls —
originally the Swann Pharmacy

TEAL (now Air New Zealand)
flying boat leaving Suva for Apia, 1960

until she was more than seventeen. Swann was as strict as most other fathers of the period. Boy friends for a sixteen-year-old were just not permissible, but Maggie was this age when she was smitten with true love at first sight.

Strolling down Beach Road one evening on her way to music she glimpsed young Peter Fabricius who had just arrived home from New Zealand. As their eyes met Maggie says she knew immediately this stranger would become her husband. Peter, nearly twenty, the son of a pioneer settler, was born in 1889 at So'otu in Falealili. His father, also named Peter, was from the island of Marstal in Denmark. His mother was Phoebe, the daughter of an early American trader Benjamin Allen and his Samoan wife Miliama of Falealili. In those early days Falealili vied strongly with Apia as a trading port for overseas vessels calling at Samoa.

Maggie did not see Peter again for nearly two years, when he came home in 1910 to assume control of the family business after the death of his father.

There followed so many secret meetings that it was thought high time Maggie Swann and Peter Fabricius were officially introduced. The couple continued to meet as often as possible. Although Peter was very busy in his new business role, it was no surprise to the locals when they were married in 1913, Maggie aged twenty and her husband twenty-four.

*   *   *

On August 6, 1914, news reached Samoa of the entry of Great Britain into World War I. It was transmitted by the newly constructed Telefunken-type wireless located in the mountains some six miles from Apia. Only completed in July it was somewhat ironical that the first news it broadcast was the outbreak of the conflict that spelled the end of German rule in Samoa.

The Governor of that time, Dr. Erich Schultz, regarded the war seriously and immediately took action to ensure that the British and Chinese nationals remained peaceful. Acting-Consul Trood was told that British subjects would not be molested provided they were not antagonistic.

Unknown to the German Administration the Secretary of State in London cabled the Governor of New Zealand informing him that "if your Ministers desire and feel themselves able to seize the German wireless station at Samoa we should feel that this was a great and urgent Imperial service. You will realise, however, that any territory now occupied must at the conclusion of the war be at the disposal of the Imperial Government for the purposes of an ultimate settlement. Other Dominions are acting on the same understanding in a similar way."

The German years had not only given a great boost to the agricultural economy of Samoa but the Kaiser's administrators had also earned substantial revenue for the Fatherland. There had never been a published statement of the financial status of German Samoa, no doubt for the very good reason that knowledge of the considerable surplus would have fomented more troubles in the colony.

During 1911 and 1912 large revenue profits were shipped to Germany in the form of gold. On one occasion in 1912 it is believed a quarter of a million in gold marks left Apia consigned to Berlin.

The Germans realised that it was only a matter of time before an Allied occupation force would reach the islands. Meanwhile Governor Schultz released another of his diplomatic peace-keeping bulletins: "Now, Samoa is of no influence in European affairs. There will be much naval warfare, but the war on land will decide, and not that on the sea. If tomorrow or any other day any change should come to Samoa, do not be misled into thinking that will be the end of the war. The result will be decided by the war in Europe, and not here in Samoa."

Chapter 5
World War I (1914-1918)

The New Zealand "capture" of German Samoa was not a very exciting affair. In all probability the Germans had a planned strategy ready for the day when a warship arrived in Apia Harbor.

After receiving the suggestion from the Secretary for State in London that they could perhaps capture the radio station, the New Zealanders moved with unexpected rapidity. A force of nearly 1400 volunteers was enlisted from all walks of life.

With the briefest of training they found themselves bound for Samoa via Noumea and Suva. The convoy with a Royal Australian Navy escort had steamed an indirect course of 2500 miles before anchoring in Apia Harbor on August 29, 1914.

An old Navy custom that British warships never carry a white flag caused unexpected delays to the landing group calling for the surrender of Apia. Rules of war demand the carriage of a flag of truce by such a party but there was none on board. The problem was solved by nailing a serviette to a length of timber.

Not only was there no resistance from the Germans but the Imperial Governor was absent from Apia as part of his plan to refuse a surrender. The New Zealand landing party from the little cruiser *Psyche* was confronted with minor officials who regretted they had no authority to act in such important matters as a surrender.

Their protestations fell on deaf ears as the New Zealanders cared little whether or not the Governor greeted them. Takeover of the radio station presented the occupiers with few problems, but the resourceful Germans had hidden several vital components necessary to operate the diesel engines.

Fortunately the parts were found in thick bush not far from the location. This followed the posting of a generous reward for their recovery by any soldier. Possibly a certain degree of persuasion was used at this stage otherwise it is hardly likely the hiding place would have been discovered.

Had the Germans thought of throwing the parts into nearby Lake Lanuto'o then it is almost certain they would still be rusting there to this day.

The New Zealand technicians quickly had the radio station bearing messages to and from Government headquarters in Wellington.

Making the most of their isolated occupation it was not long before the New Zealanders published their own newspaper called *The Pull-Thro*. Six numbers of this so-called "unofficial organ of the advance party" are valuable collectors' pieces today.

Towards the end of 1914 the Union Steamship Company of New Zealand which had long provided the only regular steam service to Western Samoa opened a branch in Apia.

The German population of Samoa was interned without much delay much to the disappointment of Aggie who was at the time engaged to a "handsome young German fellow."

"I was very sad," recalled Aggie, "for we had decided to marry as soon as possible. We all had many friends amongst the Germans."

After the death of his wife Pele, Swann married Fa'afeti from Apia village. There were two children, Fred and Daisy, from this union. Head of his highly respected and growing family the hard working chemist still found time to take an active part in many communal activities in Apia.

The New Zealand occupation which naturally favoured British subjects, be they planters or traders, proved helpful to Swann. He secured several lucrative contracts with the army, supplying them with remedies that were unavailable in the troops' dispensaries.

Aggie, seventeen at the time of the New Zealand occupation, told me that the Kiwis received a great welcome. It seemed to the Samoans that the war was over when overseas the four-year struggle was really only beginning.

The first years of the New Zealand occupation were not particularly eventful. Probably the greatest excitement was caused when the German heavy cruisers, the *Gneisenau* and *Scharnhorst* appeared just off the entrance to Apia Harbor. Much to the consternation of the worried shore watchers, many guns seemed ominously trained on the township.

Possibly the commanders decided that the Apia fortifications were of so little concern to the Imperial Navy that it would be a waste of ammunition to open fire and after all there were still German nationals on the island.

In 1915 the Bank of New Zealand opened a branch in Apia, bringing modern banking methods to the country for the first time. It was also in 1915 that the German firm DH & PG was placed in military receivership. By the end of 1916 all other German trading concerns of any importance were closed and their assets liquidated.

The Swann family now occupied a prominent position in the social life of Apia. Maggie, Aggie and Mary were still known as the Swann bouquet — and the envy of the eligible male population, although Maggie had recently married.

Samoa's most severe earthquake was on June 26, 1917, and a few days later it was vividly described in the *Samoa Times*:-

"The first effects were felt at 6.23 p.m. when the inhabitants of Apia and district were startled by the vibrations which for the first few seconds caused little alarm. Buildings shook violently, iron roofs rattled, ornaments, glasses, crockery on shelves toppled and the ground rocked in a most alarming manner.

"Although the people were greatly disturbed many took the wise precaution of extinguishing all lights. Those in rooms above the ground level experienced a new sensation in their endeavour to walk down the stairs which oscillated violently in awkward positions."

The paper reported that strong nerved men stood dumbfounded as the earth rocked beneath them. Women and children screamed and fainted. At Savalolo Samoans were observed to pray.

The shocks extended over a period of about two minutes, the experience was terrifying. Late at night when the severe vibrations ceased people stood in groups outside their houses but only a few ventured to bed.

The paper said residents in Samoa "were accustomed to interesting quakes, occasionally sufficiently pronounced to excite comment at the time but which were speedily forgotten."

The chief of the Observatory in Apia was Professor

Angenheister. He pinpointed the origin of the earthquake a distance of 60 to 80 miles in a south-westerly direction, and considered the Safata district may have received the main force of the disturbance. The magnitude of the force was registered as 8.3 on the Richter Scale.

Discussing damage to stores in Beach Road, the *Samoa Times* reported "Probably Messrs. Nelson & Son have been the greatest losers, the main part of the damage occurring in a room on the upper level where the crockery is stored. Here valuable glass and china were thrown down and destroyed, the approximate loss amounting to about £50. Mr. Swann the chemist, also had considerable losses to report. An inspection of his premises after the dread occurrence revealed the shop floor strewn with broken bottles, powdered drugs, lozenges and liquids, the pungent odour of iodine being particularly noticeable."

At the time of the earthquake Aggie and her father were alone in the house. The Swanns were then living in the building which is today known as Aggie's Store. Mary, Maggie and Willie were all out of the country on holidays. When the first quake struck nineteen-year-old Aggie was taking a shower.

When she felt the initial shocks, Aggie recalled, she looked up at the outlet rose of the shower and it appeared to be moving from side to side. Actually the building itself was swaying. Her father, a few rooms away, realised what was happening and called immediately, "It's an earthquake, get out of the house."

Dripping with water, Aggie grabbed her *lavalava* and made a dash through the house. Bottles, plates, and everything loose was falling to the ground. She was terrified, having never experienced anything of this magnitude. She did not know the strength of the earthquake and how much damage could result.

As Aggie made a dash through the house her *lavalava*, which had not been particularly securely tied, caught on the arm of a chair where it stayed as Aggie continued on her way, dodging falling bottles and intent only on getting out of the back door as quickly as possible.

"Coloured waters, perfumes, liniments, everything imaginable were spread out in every room of the chemist building," said Aggie, describing the chaos. "I raced through the house and out into the backyard where father immediately reproached me for my appearance. I dashed back into the house and quickly wrapped myself in a towel. Despite the gravity of the situation father said the Swann girls should never ever appear that way in public!"

At the British Club, next door to the Swann home, and at Andrew and Syddall, there were also a number of breakages of falling bottles and the like. The *Samoa Times* graphically described how "a number of cavities occurred in the ground in the residential area. In the grounds of Mr. N. H. MacDonald at Vaiala a huge hole measuring about 30 ft. square was seen."

A great tidal wave followed the quake. At Aleipata it was described as sweeping in with a white wall of foam ten feet high. Several people were reported drowned.

On Savai'i several bridges and churches were severely damaged.

Reports reaching Apia in the next couple of weeks included rumors that an island had emerged from the ocean some 80 miles west of Savai'i, also that the volcano was once more in eruption.

"These reports," said the newspaper, "do not appear to have been confirmed."

*　　*　　*

57

There had never been a shortage of suitors awaiting the Swann girls, Aggie told me. As often as possible there were gatherings of family friends who were all closely united during the war years. Aggie enjoyed the company of many of the eligible bachelors but did not fall in love until she met Gordon Hay-Mackenzie, a handsome New Zealander.

Hay-Mackenzie came to Samoa to work with the New Zealand Trust Estates taking over the former German plantations. Later he was appointed to manage the office of the Union Steamship Company, a pioneer shipping line plying between New Zealand and the islands. His position as manager was socially important and financially lucrative.

"The status symbol in those days," as described by Aggie, "was a shining buggy drawn by a frisky pony. Gordon had a beautiful buggy topped with a colorful frieze which I vividly remember.

"Together we would drive down Beach Road, me in a long flowing dress and Gordon in his white tropical suit. They were grand times."

After a short courtship and at the age of twenty, Aggie decided to marry Hay-Mackenzie.

"Father was happy with the match," Aggie explained. "He arranged a big reception despite the shortage of many commodities caused by the war, for this was the year 1917.

"In those days," laughed Aggie, " we had to be really thoroughly married. There were three wedding services. The religious ceremony was at the Apia Protestant Church in Beach Road near where my hotel is now located. My bridesmaids were Gladys Newton and Dora Tattersall, two of the most beautiful and dutiful attendants that one could have wished for."

Aggie and Gordon went through a ceremony to

marry them under New Zealand laws. They had to repeat the service in a different form to be registered under Samoan regulations.

"There's no doubt we were well and truly married," said Aggie, who then recalled the grand reception that was held at the residence of Mr. Graff in the hills above Apia at Papasa'e.

"In the German days this place was called the 'Sanatorium of Samoa' where Europeans went to rest and enjoy the mountain air," continued Aggie.

"Herr Decker used to advertise his 125-acre farm as a perfect 'paradise for health and quietude seekers'.

"This was back in 1905," Aggie proved as she produced a newspaper clipping in which the German settler publicised his sanatorium complete with a vegetable garden, twelve cows providing fresh milk, butter and cheese. There was fishing and swimming in the Vaisigana River which ran through the estate. With such bracing mountain air guests needed blankets almost every night, the advertisement warned.

In 1918 during the time that the severe influenza epidemic was sweeping the world, Aggie was waiting in New Zealand for the *Talune* to sail to Samoa. The 'flu was raging in New Zealand and this was the ship that transported the disease to Western Samoa.

When the *Talune* sailed on October 30, everybody aboard the ship was scared of the disease. Aggie was no exception.

"Soon I was so sick I was sure I was going to die," she recalled. "The doctors told me later I was lucky to be alive. We landed in Apia on November 8 and the passengers moved out amongst their families. Quickly the 'flu spread far and wide through the islands. The Samoans had no resistance to such a severe European virus and died in thousands.

"My father and Dr. Atkinson worked night and day until they collapsed from fatigue. The 'flu didn't effect Pago because the authorities placed a strict quarantine on American Samoa. It was one of the few countries that escaped the epidemic."

The disease raged unabated in Western Samoa mainly because there was an acute shortage of drugs. Aggie's father and Dr. Atkinson continued to treat the sufferers but death took a tremendous toll. It was said an offer of unlimited drugs and a team of doctors from American Samoa were refused for some obscure reason in Apia by Colonel Robert Logan, the Administrator.

People were dying so fast that there were just not sufficient able bodied men to bury them. For a time burning the dead was the only way to quickly dispose of the victims. Needless to say this method was not very popular in Samoa so the Administrator decided to approach the problem differently.

He gathered together all the Germans and Solomon Islanders (black boys, as they were called) pointing out to them that they were to become an important cog in his plan to defeat the epidemic.

Logan set them to work digging a huge pit near the church at Vaimosa. When the excavation was complete the Solomom Islanders were sent to gather the bodies which lay in shacks and *fales* through the Apia area. They were to be laid out *en bloc* for a mass burial. This way the colonel hoped to catch up with the disposal of the back log of bodies.

The Solomon Islanders, who needed considerable persuasion to set about their morbid task, were generally given a couple of nobblers of whisky to make their work appear less unpleasant.

On one occasion it was reported the corpse collectors went to a *fale* where there was a Chinaman stretched out. They gathered up his body and quickly transferred it to the pit. The Chinaman apparently was the last in a line of bodies arraigned ready for burial. As the black boys were shovelling some lime over him preparatory to a layer of soil the Chinaman came to life. He took one look around him, leapt out of the pit and ran off at top speed.

Armed with shovels and picks the Solomon Islanders gave chase shouting "The doctor says you are dead so you must be dead. Stop, so that we can bury you in the proper way."

Fortunately the effects of the whisky slowed the black boys who gave up the pursuit. Had they caught the escaping Chinaman there is little doubt he would have been hit over the head and put back in the pit to be buried "according to instructions".

It is officially estimated that 7,542 Samoans died during the epidemic. During one of the most virulent periods Swann's second wife Fa'afeti was stricken. Despite all attempts by her husband and the over-worked Doctor Atkinson, she died when urgently needed drugs which would have saved the lives of thousands were only eighty miles away in Pago Pago.

The text of the message offering help from American Samoa was made public at an official enquiry after the epidemic had abated. It read:—

"Greatly distressed to hear of seriousness of epidemic — Please advise me if we can be of any service or assistance. From Governor J. M. Poyer."

The telegram was addressed to the American Consulate in Apia. Consul Mitchell in Apia said he showed the message to Colonel Logan.

One of the findings of the investigation was that a Reverend Paul Cane had the disease when the *Talune* left New Zealand and that he was the cause of spreading it through the ship.

Evidence was given that the New Zealand health authorities failed to advise Samoa of the epidemic proportions.

The official death toll was horrifying:—

Population before epidemic:—

Upolu	23,955	38,178
Savai'i	14,223	

After epidemic:—

Upolu	19,129	30,636
Savai'i	11,507	

Deaths:—

men	3,265
women	2,704
children	1,573
	7,542

When Dr. Atkinson gave the *Talune* a health clearance in Apia on November 8 he little realised he and chemist Swann were to be confronted with the worst scourge ever to strike Western Samoa.

*   *   *

From Aggie's marriage with Gordon Hay-MacKenzie there were four children. Peggy died from tuberculosis at the age of 21, Ian succumbed as an infant at 20 months, and Pele, named after Aggie's mother, died in New Zealand in 1976. Gordon who is the sole survivor lives in New Zealand and visited Apia for a family reunion in October, 1972.

Late in 1925 Aggie's first husband was stricken with tuberculosis. Hoping for a recovery, he went to New Zealand to stay with his brother, a bank manager, at Hawera, a borough in the North Island provincial district of Taranaki. Gordon Hay-MacKenzie died there early in 1926.

Chapter 6
The Difficult Years (1919-1929)

The twelve months that followed the Armistice in 1918 was to bring many changes to Western Samoa, resulting in greater discontent than had occurred during the entire four years of war.

Unhappily the Samoans found themselves in an unenviable situation, bracketed with America in the disastrous prohibition movement that had just been introduced in the United States. Western Samoa was still under New Zealand military occupation at that time and this status did not change until the Treaty of Versailles was completed in January, 1920. The virtual dictatorship of this army control gave authority to a small group of officials obviously controlled from Wellington.

History shows that New Zealand had long wanted the "colony" of Western Samoa even before the German annexation of 1899. To possibly influence the League of Nations decisions and to prove they had an effective control of the native population, the New Zealanders passed a drastic law which made the country "dry".

Very soon there began a closure of European-type hotels and clubs. There was just no liquor to sell! During the German era there were many reputable well conducted hostelries in Apia. The *Samoa Weekly Herald* of September 1, 1898 listed seven hotelkeepers. The International Hotel at Matafale, under the management of Robert Easthope, had an advertisement in the same newspaper. It boasted an upstairs verandah for one hundred people and offered first class accommodation for 'tourists and others who may visit Samoa.'

Easthope roamed the world until he found himself in the South Pacific. He was born in Cumberland, England in 1848 and at an early age was apprenticed to the sea.

After serving his time, young Robert eventually became quarter-master of the cable steamer *Omeo*, sailing the New Zealand coasts.

In his early forties Easthope decided it was time to leave the sea and settle down in one of the glamourous South Sea island groups.

His first choice was Tonga where for some years he managed trading stations. Tiring of the trader's monotonous life of continually seeing the same faces, Easthope yearned for a more active existence. He wanted to stay in the Pacific but preferred to be among the cosmopolitan crowds that frequented the fanciful South Sea island ports.

Bob came to Apia in 1894 only to lose all his belongings in a huge fire that swept the town.

By 1896 he had recovered from the effects of the calamity and in February managed his first inn, the Club Hotel. Next move was to the Tivoli Hotel where he remained until he opened a hotel at Malifa.

When Easthope became manager of the International Hotel he controlled the most popular hotel in Apia. Although it is difficult to imagine many tourists visiting Samoa in the 1890s there were plenty arriving by ships from New Zealand, Germany and America.

Publicity for the International always emphasised the hotel's popularity with tourists — "the dining, drawing, and bedrooms detached from the main building or bar area."

Bob Easthope was doing very well; owning a nice residential property overlooking the town and operating a lucrative livery stable.

He catered for commercial travellers stressing the hotel's central location — the post office on one side, the customs house and the DH & PG building on the other.

Known to everyone as "Obliging Bob" because of his kind manners Easthope ferried his guests to their ships in the harbour by his own boats. At the time of his death on December 16, 1932 at the age of 84, he was the oldest British resident in Samoa.

Aggie was born in the family home right opposite the International Hotel in Beach Road. As a child she little knew how important the old building would become in her future life. In fact there was only great relief when one day the three Swann girls saw workmen dismantling the hotel.

They mentioned to their father that the carpenters seemed to be so very careful not to damage any of the timber. "Yes," he replied, "you are quite right. Mr. Hetherington has bought the building. They are taking special pains with the demolition. It is going to be re-erected down by the Vaisigano River."

Aggie said: "Many a time I watched 'Obliging Bob' welcome patrons at the International Hotel. Little did I realise that I would step into his shoes to greet my own customers in that very same hotel re-built at the other end of Beach Road."

The hotel was soon re-built using the same front and with two stories, looking just as it did at the previous site. Despite storm and tempest the facade of the historical building has retained its original appearance. Outwardly then the International Hotel is much the same today as it was in the 1870s when slave traders like Bully Hayes swaggered down the Beach to drink at their favourite tables in a bar that was renowned throughout the South Seas. The hotel is now more widely known through the Pacific as Aggie Grey's.

Going "dry" under the New Zealand control effected the European and the Samoan population in different ways. In those days the *papalagi* traders were known as the "Beach" because they not only traded almost exclusively on Beach Road but they gathered on the esplanade to air their grievances.

Today it is not much different — practically all of Samoa's commercial and Government headquarters are either on Beach Road or a stone's throw away. Only now there is no worry of prohibition — occasionally some shortages of favourite imported brands, but that's all.

When the oceans of beer and champagne and whisky that had flowed continuously dried up, protests began in deadly earnest. During the German occupation there were no serious protests by the Beach — their semi-intoxicated state left the traders' grievances only half expressed.

The 1919 situation can be likened to the mental state of a heavy smoker or a drinker who has become virtuous. Denying himself these vices he becomes positively unbearable, sometimes unreasonable for varying lengths of time. All sorts of allegations were thrown at the New Zealand administration. "Look at what they are doing," was the cry, "they give us a new water supply and what we want is whisky."

The hospital staff had been greatly increased to control the two troublesome tropical diseases, hookworm and elephantitis. "This is a waste of money," challenged the Beach, "everybody knows that the Germans left the filaria to follow their own simple ways in the bloodstream — and who knows that this was not the correct way?"

They also protested that "New Zealand has dared to keep to the letter of the German contract with Chinese coolies and the Solomon Island black boys. They are repatriating them before we can get new coolies from Hong Kong. We will have no labor for the plantations — things will get worse and worse."

Although at the time these protests had nothing to do with the *Mau* movement it is certain prohibition fomented the troubles that followed in the next decade. The Beach were quick to realise that they could never hope to gain a Samoan independence by direct appeal to the League of Nations or the British Government. Somehow they would have to prove to the League that the New Zealand administration was rotten to the core — far beyond redemption.

Following the World War I victory a friendly Japan was extending her empire southwards taking over mandate of a huge area of the central Pacific including the German colonies. Perhaps a rumour of "Japan spreading still further" might convince the League to remove Samoa from New Zealand control thought the Beach. But this plan was considered too difficult to organise.

It was widely understood that the League's intentions were to protect the people living in the mandated territories, especially the natives of the countries effected. Here was the greatest problem for the Europeans — the Beach formed only a very small part of the population of Samoa and would certainly be considered of secondary importance in any decision making.

Drinking was to become a problem.

Most countries of the world have always had some form of intoxicant be it in drug form or liquid. Previously the Polynesians had never cultivated anything stronger than *kava* which is non-intoxicating. When left standing the liquid does not ferment but depreciates into a stale and rather unpalatable drink. Freshly prepared *kava* is an acquired taste for Europeans, quite pleasant to those who enjoy the beverage and harmless even if consumption becomes a habit.

Before long home brewing and distilling developed at a tremendous pace. The practice became so prevalent that the police were incapable of coping with the offences. Much of the liquor was dangerous to drink, especially a potent "cocoa juice" marketed by the Chinese.

When cocoa was harvested the beans and the white covering paste were left in bins for about three days for fermenting. After separation the flavoured beans were readily sold, leaving the white paste transformed into as potent a brew as one can imagine. The liquor was bottled and sold quite openly in the Chinese stores.

*   *   *

During this extremely unsettled period a romance was blossoming in the Swann family. On September 6, 1919, Aggie's sister Mary was married to Robert D. Croudace, chief clerk of John Rothschild and Company. The wedding was held in the Cathedral following the signing of the "civil contract" at the Court House.

Mary's bridesmaids were Dora Simpson, Eileen Fabricius, Clara Passie, and Daisy Swann. Aggie's husband Gordon and Hector Robertson attended the bridegroom. Her brother Freddie and Peter Fabricius were the train bearers.

*   *   *

In 1920 Western Samoa officially became a mandated territory of the League of Nations — on May 1, following the signing of the Treaty of Versailles in January. It was decreed that the country would be administered in trust by New Zealand.

In the month following the appointment the new rulers exercised their supreme authority with a somewhat sordid decree directed at local pure-blood Germans. These settlers and their families were served with deportation orders to return to Germany. As those married to Samoans were exempted from the new law, a large number of quickly arranged weddings considerably reduced the list of eligibles.

Even so there were still 170 proud people uprooted from their homes in Samoa bound for Germany, many for the first time. They travelled on the s.s. *Main* which arrived in the harbour on June 13, 1920.

"Like most ships at that time there was influenza on board," Aggie recalled, "No one could forecast whether the terrible epidemic would flare up and spread through the ship. The s.s. *Main* could have become a floating deathtrap.

"Customs officers searched the passengers for currency — a crafty German was discovered with English pound notes tucked in the brim of his hat. Another had a watchchain of gold sovereigns and a five pound gold coin.

"The government launch *Tahutu* towed lighters carrying the passengers from the wharf at 4 p.m. Before they had gone twenty yards they burst into

69

song with Deutschland Uber Alles, continuing all the way out to the *Main*."

Many of the Europeans left in Apia did not agree with the deportation according to newspaper reports. There were mixed feelings. Some said, "Well, the Germans have gone, for good or ill." Most agreed however that "under the German rule they gave us a good run."

Provided he had a credit in Samoa each male deportee was given £100 plus a proportionate allowance for his children. Altogether the passengers on the *Main* took with them 140,000 German marks to begin their lives afresh.

Other personal possessions left behind were to be valued and compensation eventually sent to Germany.

"It was quite a sad time," reflected Aggie, "because we all had good friends among the Germans. Possibly we would never see them again."

Tourism has always been in the minds of Samoan traders. Since the beginning of the German days the possibilities have been discussed. Genuine tourists can be counted upon to bring much-needed foreign currency to any country. It is to the credit of the governments of Western Samoa that tourism has never taken over the country as has happened to other parts of the Pacific. The Samoans were lucky for somehow that "controlled tourism" worked. It worked because of certain circumstances, accidental or well considered which prevented the influx of outsiders.

In 1920 when tourist attractions were featured in the local press, the question arose of access roads to Lake Lanuto'o, said to be one of the best spots in Western Samoa.

The local editor emphasised "that in the German days Lake Lanuto'o was in regular use. They (the

Germans) built two houses and supplied a rowing boat with funds contributed by residents. In 1919 it was suggested a motor road be built.

"Up to Tapatapao there's a motor road. A further stretch of road running to Schroeder's plantation would require little expense to make it good. Beyond Schroeder's place the distance to the ridge is only 2,000 yards and the ground is as level as a table. The grades are very low from Tapatapao to Falemauga and Lanuto'o,'being not more than 1 in 20 or 25."

Aggie described Lake Lanuto'o as a beautiful place. "The Germans went there for weekends," she said. "It was ideal for swimming, boating and fishing. The only drawback was the mosquitoes. Not only were they so prevalent, but some were reported to be as big as locusts, and to have an appetite just as large," laughed Aggie.

In 1920 the first member of the British Royal Family to visit Western Samoa arrived in HMS *Renown*. The Prince of Wales as he was then, later to become King Edward VIII and after abdication retitled the Duke of Windsor, received a warm reception from the Samoan people.

"The Prince was a handsome gentleman," said Aggie, "and Samoa gave him a traditional welcome. To us the *Renown* was an immensely impressive warship with a tremendous number of sailors. Times then were very exciting. The New Zealanders were in occupation, the Germans had gone, and we had our first English royal visitor."

The Treaty of Versailles in January, 1920, and the decisions that followed had resulted in Western Samoa becoming a mandated territory in the care of New Zealand. Six years later in 1926 the nationalist movement, the *Mau*, again exploded.

Discontent had been simmering for the past two

years, but the movement had lacked an outspoken organiser as a leader. Collectively the movement had voiced the Samoans' intense resentment at their country being ruled by another.

New Zealand provided administrators who made countless mistakes, the worst example probably was the appointment in 1923 of Major-General George Richardson. The Samoans did not relish a continuation of what appeared to them to be a rule of wartime regimentation. They wanted a measure of say in the running of their land. It was a case, the Samoans said, of a trustee territory being slavishly treated like a colony and this wasn't the intention of the League of Nations.

*   *   *

In 1926 Aggie married Charlie Grey at the Apia Protestant Church in Beach Road just a few steps from her present store and hotel. Visitors to Samoa are familiar with the striking contrasts of architecture used in the construction of the hundreds of churches that serve the religious fervour of the 160,000 inhabitants.

The Apia Protestant has a design all of its own. The old-style wooden architecture is said to be the only one of that type in Samoa.

From the marriage there were three children — Maureen now living in Australia, Edward living in New Zealand and Alan who is the manager of the hotel.

*   *   *

The Samoans by now had found a true leader in Olaf Frederick Nelson. In 1910 under German rule Nelson had been a party to a petition to Berlin, in part complaining of inadequate local representation.

Now sixteen years later he was to become involved in a long, bitter struggle against what the *Mau* considered unfair rule by New Zealand.

Olaf Frederick Nelson was born in Savai'i on February 24, 1884. His father, August Nelson was born in Sweden in 1838. The year 1864 found him trying his luck in the diggings in New Zealand.

In 1868 the lure of the tropics brought August to Savai'i where he immediately opened a trading post.

By 1872 he was firmly established at Safune, Savai'i, owning the largest and best stocked store. He also operated a successful business in Apia. August married a beautiful Samoan girl, Sina, from the village of Tugaga.

August was known for his frequently voiced opinion of the Samoans — "Treat them as men and they'll treat you the same." Obviously a very good philosophy, for August Nelson suffered no losses during the Samoan wars.

Frederick, classed by law a European, worked for the German firm DH & PG for a time, then joined his father's business.

In 1909 he was married to Rosie, a daughter of the well-known American trader Harry Jay Moors, whose wife was a Samoan.

O. F. Nelson had six daughters, and a son who died as a result of the flu epidemic. Today his descendants are spread far and wide in Samoa and overseas. In Beach Road the name O. F. Nelson remains prominent in the stores that line the waterfront.

Nelson, a student of Samoan legends, has during the twentieth century been responsible for some of the deepest research into the folklore of his people.

He gave many lectures on the subject and on occasions wrote at length about his findings.

The high title of Taisi was bestowed on O.F. through his mother's family connections. This title, specially honoured as being descended from the first Tupua, brought him into the group known as *alo-ali'i* (sons of the chief).

In 1926 Nelson commenced publication of the *Samoa Guardian*. Printed in purple ink to match the *Mau* colours it was the first newspaper in the Samoan language.

The long battle between the *Mau* and the New Zealanders continued. Banishment and imprisonment became the regular method of silencing protesters.

At a 1927 Parliamentary enquiry in Wellington, Nelson and Apia trader A. G. Smyth attended. It was decided that a Royal Commission be held to enquire into the Samoan problems. The Commission ruled in favour of the administration.

With the undoubted backing of these findings the New Zealand Government ordered the deportation from Samoa of Smyth for two years, O. F. Nelson and E. W. Gurr for five years each. Gurr was married to Fanua, daughter of the chief of Apia village.

The *Samoa Guardian* was banned, only to reappear printed in Auckland.

The *Mau* seemed to gain in strength rather than become depressed by the blows dealt the movement through the deportations. Their actions in Apia appeared to follow a pattern of continually frustrating the Administration — O.F. was dictating the policy from faraway Auckland.

The situation became so tense that the New Zealand cruisers *Diomede* and *Dunedin* were called to Apia to restore order.

The Beach Road stores were then being picketed by the Samoans and surprisingly included the firm of O. F. Nelson. It was rumoured this instruction might have come from O.F. himself so there would be no appearance of favouritism.

More likely, however, it was an indication that the Samoans were bracketing the traders with the administrators in their fight for the salvation of their ideals.

A force of 74 New Zealand policemen had arrived in Apia to maintain law and order. Some were billeted at the British Club, now Aggie's Hotel.

I asked Aggie about this tense period in Samoan history. She wasn't anxious to talk of the unhappy days.

"Of course, we often saw the policemen going and returning to the British Club because father lived next door." She said "The Club was right where my hotel is now. I always worried that the situation might get out of hand and there would be some terrible bloodshed. Unfortunately this is exactly what did happen."

The two-year deportation order against A. G. Smyth had finished and the Apia merchant was expected home early in the morning of December 28, 1929. He was travelling on the s.s. *Lady Roberts* accompanied by Mr. Hall-Skelton, the lawyer representing O. F. Nelson.

Arrangements had been made for a large body of *Mau* representing all parts of the country to accord a traditional welcome to Smyth immediately he set foot on the shore. This was to be followed in the afternoon by an official *Mau* function at Vaimoso.

At 6 a.m. a group of 700 Samoans led by a uniformed brass band marched from Vaimoso into Apia. Prominently displayed was the purple with white border *Mau* flag. From the other side of the town another party of 700 marched to join their comrades at the Tivoli wharf, landing point for the ship's launch.

When the Vaimoso group reached the Courthouse on Beach Road eight members of the New Zealand police had the marchers under surveillance. These zealous observers spotted several "wanted men" in the procession. Armed only with batons the police attempted to arrest them.

This was possibly the most unfortunate decision ever made in the long New Zealand-Samoa relations. Had these police tactfully decided not to interfere the terrible tragedy that followed would not have happened. When the New Zealand police broke the ranks of the marchers the Samoans retaliated the only way possible, using their sticks and stones to protect their comrades.

A reinforcement of 20 uniformed New Zealand police arrived armed with revolvers. The police were forced to retreat, split into two parties, one around the Courthouse corner at Ifi Ifi street and the other into Mrs. P. C. Fabricius storeyard.

The swelling crowd of excited Samoans forced the New Zealanders back to the police station. The air was filled with flying stones as the police emptied their revolvers into the marchers. Some of the *Mau* were already dead before the retreat by the police and many were wounded.

As a last resort the police mounted a Lewis machine gun and opened fire. It was reported that rifles with dum dum bullets were also used to drive back the Samoans.

High Chief Tamasese Lealofi was killed in the tragic affray which took the lives of eleven Samoans and one policeman. Hundreds of *Mau* injured in the battle were taken by their comrades to the villages of Vaimoso and Le'auva'a.

The Administration sent an urgent request for the cruiser HMS *Dunedin*. For several months land parties and a seaplane dropping "Surrender" messages combed the villages for wanted men. Commodore Blake of the *Dunedin* was accused of declaring war on the Samoan people.

The prestige of the New Zealand administration in the control of their Trust territory must have dropped to the lowest possible ebb as the year 1929 came to a bloody close. The Samoans could readily be excused for ridiculing the League of Nations 1920 formula that the mandate given New Zealand was to "protect the people living in the mandated territories, especially the natives of the countries effected."

Chapter 7

The Early Thirties (1930-1935)

At their lovely home in a select part of Vailima Road, Charlie and Aggie Grey entertained more than fifty friends to a New Year's Eve party. It was a fancy dress dance that proved to be one of the most popular of the many parties always held in Apia to herald the new year.

"We had some wonderful times in the early thirties", recalled Aggie. "It was a case of making our own fun. In those days for only a small expense people could provide appetising Samoan food that was enjoyed by everyone. Only the liquor was so costly and difficult to obtain."

Samoan tropical fruit is renowned for a delicious flavour especially the pineapple and the pawpaw.

"Few locals will remember that the pawpaw had other uses apart from being a food," said Aggie, describing how the tapping and curing of papain was practiced in Samoa from some years after World War I.

"The pawpaws were grown on cocoa plantations where they were tended by the regular coolies employed on the properties. In 1931 the Chinese were paid 3/6d a day (35 cents), the same wage as they had been given in the earlier more prosperous years," Aggie continued.

"The pawpaw was lightly scratched and from these incisions a white latex ran into catchment basins. The daily quota of one worker was about 6 to 8 lbs. The papain was then dried on sheets of glass in a kerosene heated drier for about 24 hours at a low even temperature.

"Until 1929 the Samoan papain brought good prices on the US and German markets, but at the onset of the depression the demand ceased and commercial marketing stopped forever."

Like all other ports in the South Seas, Apia has had its share of unusual characters — some flamboyant, some swashbuckling like Bully Hayes, others who are seldom spoken of but their presence is made important by quiet deeds and downright friendliness.

Fred Fairman at Aggie's is such a downright friendly person.

The regular visitors to Aggie's — the commercial travellers, representatives, and semi-permanent guests — know Fred. You'll see them together having a drink at the bar, but the tourist passing through doesn't get to know him. It is a pity.

Fred Fairman came to Samoa in 1931 to build the new £70,000 Burns, Philp store on Beach Road. The building carries a date of 1932 and was officially opened on June 5, 1934. Following its completion Fred went into partnership with another man, building furniture. They operated together for some years when the partnership was dissolved.

Soon afterwards Fred went to work at Aggie's doing what probably could be called superintendent of building operations and maintenance. He has been there ever since and is the one behind the scenes in the maintenance of the hotel. He is well-versed in almost every phase of building repairs, including plumbing. In fact there's hardly any problem that cannot be handled by Fred and his team of assistants.

After the death of Charlie Grey in 1943, Fred became more and more involved in the maintenance of the hotel. It must be said that Aggie's is one of the best kept hotels in the South Pacific. If anything is found to be wrong, a faulty tap, a flywire screen, a burnt out electric bulb, then it will be attended to immediately.

In many other parts of the South Pacific one can visit a hotel three months later and still find faults that were there on the last visit. Not so at Aggie's, and much credit for this maintenance must go to Fred Fairman. He is constantly on the job filtering the swimming pool water and doing all the other things needed to keep the hotel up to scratch.

Each year around Christmas time when the Samoan climate is at its worst Aggie goes to New Zealand for two or three months — Fred goes too.

The visitor to Apia is often astounded by the tremedous girth of many Samoans. Aggie blames their huge intake of food — often the wrong type, for the prolific overweight problems of men and women.

"If only they ate less of the starchy foods like taro they would be healthier," she stressed, "so much banana and bread fruit and then they sleep when really more hard work would keep their weight down to a reasonable level."

The death was recorded in November 1931 of one of the heaviest known Samoan women. She was Pii Moamanu the 37 stone (518 lbs) wife of Chief Moamanu. When she died at the age of 38 Pii was 6 feet 7 inches and could only rise and walk a few steps with extreme difficulty.

"I remember the Chief's wife", gestured Aggie, "she was a tremendous woman. I also recollect that Moamanu was fined by the court for illegally burying his wife in the backyard. Despite his plea to the court that costs to transport the huge remains of Pii to the cemetery were beyond his financial resources, the chief was fined £2 ($4).

"I'm not sure," said Aggie, "whether Pii was allowed to rest in the family backyard or if she was removed to the cemetery."

*   *   *

The year 1930 had brought a continuation of the "police action" against the *Mau*. The cruiser *Dunedin* carried a seaplane which scoured the countryside dropping messages on the villages exhorting wanted Samoans to surrender to the authorities. This Moth aircraft was the first British plane to be seen over Apia.

Fiame Faumuina was president of the *Mau* but was never arrested by the New Zealand police.

"It seemed," said Aggie, "that Faumuina was a man who was honest and forthright in his aims to find a solution to the problems. The Administrator thought it best that he should continue as leader of the *Mau* movement."

Aggie can seldom be drawn into discussions of the controversial *Mau* era. She avoids politics, but has her personal views. Like many other oldtimers Aggie will talk of O. F. Nelson and his lifetime struggles to help the Samoan people achieve their independence.

At the Government inquest held early in the new year to enquire into the bloody clash of December 28 Sergeant Horatio Waterson, sergeant of police, said he fired the Lewis machine gun. He stated he was an experienced machine gunner during World War I, from September, 1916, to the armistice.

When the war ended he was sergeant-in-charge of all the guns of his company. Waterson testified he fired the gun over the heads of the Samoans in short bursts, and once into the ground, twenty to thirty yards in front of the crowd. He said he did not believe these bullets ricocheted into the crowds of Samoans.

In May, 1933, O. F. Nelson returned home to Samoa following the expiration of his deportation. The *Mau* immediately insisted he should be their spokesman but the Administrator, Brigadier General Herbert Hart, would not agree. Any dialogue between the *Mau* and the administration became impossible.

On July 1, 1933, E. W. ("Judge") Gurr died in Pago Pago. One of the *Mau* trio (Nelson, Smyth, Gurr) he had been sentenced to the same deportation as Nelson — five years. Gurr, a colourful character dedicated to independence for Western Samoa, had been a judge in American Samoa.

He died only three months after the completion of his banishment order.

Meanwhile Nelson continued to battle for the rights of Samoan-born people, that they should have a say in the administration of their country. It was a confusing confrontation between people who were called "natives" and colonial rulers who could do no wrong.

"O. F. Nelson did much more for Western Samoa than most people realise", was Aggie's summing up of a man who some say should have his statue in Beach Road. "He spent almost a lifetime fighting for the rights of our people, looking always to the time when they would gain their independence."

During November, 1933, the *Mau* leaders visited

villages and talked with the people during a comprehensive tour of Upolo and Savaii. Many appointments were made among the local people, all part of a plan for self-rule under direct control of *Mau* headquarters.

Ringleaders of these missions were imprisoned although it was obvious to the Administration that the voice of authority and direction was that of O. F. Nelson.

Police raided his home, seizing materials that allegedly linked him with the *Mau*. O.F. was charged with the crime of being associated with the unlawful body and on March 3, 1934, sentenced to eight months gaol in New Zealand to be followed on completion with an exile from Samoa of ten years.

Nelson's wife and daughters headed a deputation to the Administrator offering *ifoga*. This *fa'a-Samoa* apology and request for clemency was to no avail. It is said that O.F. had no knowledge of this approach.

Following a legal appeal to the New Zealand Supreme Court the sentence was reduced to the three weeks he had already served, but the ten year exile was upheld.

In November, 1934, Irene, daughter of O. F. Nelson, married Tamasese Moamoa, brother of Tamasese Lealofi who was killed in the *Mau* demonstration in 1929. Tupuola Taisi Efi is a son of this marriage.

*   *   *

The necessity to import coolie labour was continually stressed by the planters. In 1931 they had said the Chinese were being excessively paid at 35 cents a day.

Some who wanted Gilbert Islanders brought to

Samoa were probably unaware the Germans had experimented with these people but had returned them to the Gilberts as unsuitable for the plantation work.

On Nauru the Chinese were paid even less — 1/6d (15 cents) for digging phosphate. Then in Samoa in 1932 wages dropped to 2/- (20 cents) per day without meals and only 10 cents with meals.

The Chinese must have considered that Samoan working conditions were satisfactory or maybe they were shanghaied aboard the migrant ships which continued to arrive in Apia.

On July 27, 1934, the *Seistan* arrived with 275 Chinese after a 19-day voyage from Hong Kong. They were recruited on a promise of 1/9d (21 cents) daily. Returning to the East the *Seistan* repatriated 400 time-expired coolies.

Not all New Zealand officials were in favour of the Chinese laborers, especially the Minister of Lands (Mr. F. Langstone). When he led a "Goodwill Mission" to Samoa he emphasised he did not like Chinese and ordered all coolies to return to Hong Kong and China.

*   *   *

HRH the Duke of Gloucester may not have been popular in Australia but he received a mighty welcome when he visited Western Samoa in February, 1935.

British royalty has always been feted for it would seem that the Samoans high respect for their own royal families extends automatically to visitors of similar ranking from overseas. The Duke travelled in HMAS *Australia*, arriving on February 7 and sailing next day.

Plans had been carefully laid for the two-day visit

but the Administration need not have worried as to the spontaneous welcome the Duke was to receive.

"This was the second English Royal visitor I had seen," Aggie recalled, "and always the Samoa people are ready to welcome such important people. In those days many people from distant villages and from Manono came in *fautasi*.

"For this 1935 visit the crowds began to arrive several weeks ahead but always they had *aiga* close to Apia with whom they can live. This is the way of life with the people of Samoa. My home is your home for as long as you wish."

*   *   *

The illicit liquor problem continued through the thirties with no obvious solution in sight. The abolition of prohibition was never considered as a possibility.

As far back as January, 1932, the Administrator (General Hart) announced he favoured an official liquor importation giving an allowance to "responsible" European citizens. No mention was made of "responsible" Samoan citizens.

At that time smuggled whisky was selling at £1-£1/15/- ($2 to $3.50) a bottle.

The police made many raids on clubs holding functions but could not hope to greatly reduce the flow of illicit liquor. On April 6, 1935, the Moana Cabaret owned by Mr. E. Fabricius, was holding an "Hawaiian Night," with an admission charge of ten shillings for gentlemen and five shillings for ladies. The police raided the club seizing slygrog beer and whisky.

Besides the commencement of the new BP store, there was another happening to bring Samoa into the modern age. Early in 1931 a radio station opened in

Apia. Playing gramophone recordings the station operated on a wavelength of 320 meters and had an output of 2.5 kilowatts.

Perhaps the most important event in 1935 was the coming of talking pictures to Apia. In May General Hart performed the opening ceremony and was on the target when he prophesied that the most popular movies would feature the Wild West — and throughout Samoa, more than forty years later, they are still the most popular.

Chapter 8

Death of William Swann (1936-1941)

When Aggie's father died on May 20, 1936, it was a most severe shock to the Swann family. "Father was the head of our family," said Aggie, "and was always ready to help us with advice. We did not notice how the time was passing until when he died we realised he was 77."

Swan had been in Western Samoa for 47 years, never regretting that in 1889 it had been the South Seas island of his choice — a place to settle down and raise his family.

The Apia newspapers published glowing testimonials of his service to the Samoan people. They told of his courageous devotion to duty in the 1918 influenza epidemic, how although he was more than 60 years of age he often worked 24 hours without rest to try to save the lives of victims of the disease.

Twice in his lifetime he had met Royalty. The first time was in 1880 when he acted as an interpreter for the visit to Fiji of the Duke of Clarence and Prince George (later King George V).

When the Prince of Wales toured Western Samoa in 1920 Swann mentioned his Fijian meeting to the Prince who later became Edward VIII. After his dramatic abdication in 1938 Edward was known as the Duke of Windsor.

The newspapers reported that the pioneering pharmacist was survived by four daughters —

Mrs. P. C. Fabricius (Maggie); Mrs. C. M. Grey (Aggie); Mrs. R. D. Croudace (Mary); Mrs. H. Mann (Daisy),

and two sons —

Mr. W. M. Swann (Willie); Mr. Fred Swann.

All of the children were living in Apia. At the time of his death his only remaining brothers and sisters were Sister Mary Joseph of the Marist Sisters Convent, Mrs. H. P. St. Julian of Sydney and Mr. Herbert Swann of Levuka.

A lifetime in the South Seas had ended for a pioneer who did everything in his power to better the health of the peoples of Western Samoa — the Europeans and the Samoans, there was no difference to his way of thinking.

Probably he was lucky to live through the dreadful influenza epidemic of 1918. Subjected to the virus and frequently in a state of physical exhaustion he managed to survive. It is said that he alone probably saved the lives of hundreds, maybe thousands of Samoans who would have otherwise died when they became inflicted with the scourge.

The death of their father meant a big re-adjustment in the Swann clan. Closely knit, the family found it hard to believe that the head of the *aiga* was gone forever.

*　　*　　*

Samoan cricket, the national sport, is never dull. The unexpected performance of the three-sided bat serves to keep the spectators as well as the fielders and the batsmen in a state of suspense. The wickets, looking like spindly matchsticks, are easily skittled by the balls made from strips of raw rubber bled from local trees. The rules, also localised to suit *aiga* requirements, are a far cry from the game as played at the Melbourne Cricket Ground or Lords in London.

There is no limit to the number in each team so long as they are equal, nor to their sex, and if you have a uniform be sure to wear it. Those not batting or fielding sit together in the shade singing and dancing. When their captain blows his whistle, those fielding leap into the air with a whoop, somewhat like a Thai boxer who calls to his spirits before the fight. The Samoans flutter like birds, spin on their heels like tops, perform somersaults, all according to the number of blasts.

Unlike modern international tactics, this is not done to distract a nervous batsman facing a fast bowler, for all bowlers are fast. The captain blows his whistle just because he feels happy, maybe the best player of the opposing side has been dismissed.

Cricket matches sometimes last for several days because a defeated team can buy itself back into the competition with another entrance fee. The host village may collect $1,000 in fees but be eaten out of food, for as long as the game continues there must be an ample supply of pigs, *taro*, breadfruit, *pisupo*, bananas, or the hosts face unrelenting criticism from the visitors. The resultant shame is the worst thing that can happen to the village. So food must be always available — regardless of cost!

In Samoa, cricket is a very serious game. During one inter-village match near Apia a visiting batsman was given out when he was superbly caught by a young boy, the brother of the umpire. The singing and dancing stopped when the indignant batsman protested, rightly so because the boy was only a spectator. The umpire, proud of his young brother, adhered to his decision, and is probably the only umpire in the history of cricket to lose his life for doing so. He was killed on the field with a mighty swipe of the bat on his head. Samoan cricket is like that, the unexpected can always happen.

Retired director of the Post Office, Ernest Betham, tells the story of an event which occurred in the early days of his service when a messenger boy in the department. Part of his duties was to collect money owing to the Post Office from the Savai'i Island area.

It so happened that during the time of one of his regular trips a murder occurred on Savai'i as a result of a particularly exciting cricket match. One of the players tackled an opposing participant, wielding a bat to emphasise his opinion of the final decision. It brought about the death of one Samoan cricketer — definitely in this case a member of the winning side.

In early days there were no police courts on Savai'i so it was necessary for the case to be heard in Apia. When the cricketer was brought over to Apia and charged with the murder of the person, there was of course no actual evidence of a body. An urgent message was sent to Savai'i to pick up the dead Samoan who had been buried the next day because of the necessity in tropical areas to dispose of the corpse as soon as possible.

It would appear that the message emphasised the necessity to have evidence of the death of the particular person. After the body was exhumed the Samoans conferred and considered that it seemed a formidable task to send the body by island steamer over to Apia. It was agreed, that by cutting off the head, this particular part of the body would be sufficient proof that the cricketer was indeed dead. So with a minimum of ceremony the head was removed from the body and placed in a galvanised iron bucket in which there was a quantity of some type of chemical to effect preservation until the consignment reached Apia.

As the boat did not leave until early next morning it was necessary for the special cargo to be stored in a small enclosed waiting room in which Ernest Betham also had to bed down for the night. To this day, Ernest Betham still remembers how the non-blinking shining eyes in the bucket seemed to stare at him throughout the night. It was certain sleep did not come easy to the postal messenger boy that evening, indeed not for several nights that followed his return from Savai'i.

*　　*　　*

William, now a well-known businessman in Apia, recalled how as a boy he got his first sports coat — when employed as a junior in a general store in Beach Road. He had often admired a nicely tailored jacket in the store, but priced at £2 the beautiful coat far exceeded the spending power of a junior earning ten-shillings per week. Four weeks' work for one jacket was a decision that needed considerable thought.

William continued to admire the coat and all the staff in the store, including a departmental manager, were aware of the fact. All over the world in commercial life the junior is subject to practical jokes or acts of simple trickery to make him appear a scapegoat and a laughing stock of the rest of the staff. In Apia it was no different from other parts of the world.

One day the departmental manager saw Aggie and the owner of the shop wandering nonchalantly behind some fixtures headed for the bulk storeroom. He concluded that there might be some interesting scenes occurring later in the warm afternoon. Why should the boss enjoy this pleasure when he kept such a tight rein on the staff? Here was an opportunity, thought the manager, to cause a little interruption to their fun and gain some laughs at the expense of the junior, William.

After allowing the couple a little time to get settled, the manager called William and told him to pick up some stock from a certain section of the storeroom. Quietly and in all innocence William went on his errand as directed.

Not expecting to see anyone else in the storeroom, William was dumbfounded when he came to a sudden halt three or four feet away from the glaring face of his boss. With the situation as it was, Aggie did not see William as she had her back to him.

Nodding and shaking his head the boss indicated in no uncertain manner that he wished William to proceed as quickly as possible to any other part of the building than where he was presently standing. For a time the goggle-eyed William appeared rooted to the floor of the storeroom and just could not get moving, but when he did become mobile the junior got far away from the corner.

No fool, William quickly realised he had been framed by the manager. Possibly several Peeping Toms witnessed the situation from a distance because the manager appeared to have been quickly informed of the result of William's intrusion on the scene.

Unable to hide his mirth over the incident, the smile on the manager's face suddenly turned to a look of concern when William said, "Sir, I'm going to tell the boss that you deliberately sent me to the storeroom knowing that he was there with Aggie."

Now it was the manager's turn to do some fast thinking. Looking the junior straight in the eye he said, "William, I know that you have been admiring that coat in the showroom for quite a long time now, but you have not had sufficient money to buy it. If you would like the coat I think I can make a special price for you. I am offering you the coat at a discounted price of five shillings.

"I am sure you will want it, William, and please say so if you do. But I also feel certain you will not wish to tell the boss that I sent you to the storeroom. Agreed William?"

William agreed. He and Aggie have often laughed over the way she indirectly brought about the unexpected purchase of his first jacket.

*   *   *

New Zealand's first Labour Government was elected towards the end of 1935. When in opposition they had pledged a pardon for O. F. Nelson, together with a clearance to the *Mau* so that they were no longer an unlawful body.

In July, 1936, Nelson and his daughters returned to Apia as guests of the new government. A wind of change was blowing in Western Samoa bringing for the first time a hope of real independence. O. F. Nelson was elected as the *fa'atonu* of the *Mau*. With this appointment as consul or adviser it was proposed by the movement that he should be a nominee for the Legislative Council.

A jubilant *Mau* with their beloved organiser back with them planned many improvements. Now they could openly campaign and discuss their self-government aims without the threat of imprisonment.

In their enthusiasm the leaders were naturally

inclined to favour those officials who had been faithful members of the *Mau* movement. Many Samoans who had not been members found themselves out of office — replaced by a loyal *Mau*. To prove their allegiance even judges appeared in court dressed in the *Mau* uniform.

By 1937 the parliament of the Samoans, mainly *Mau* leaders, was still only an advisory body. The group sat for several months deliberating over the promises made to them by the Labour Government of New Zealand. The thirty-nine members were united in their demands for their *Fono*. The ultimate aim was for self-government of Samoa — this was clearly apparent, but the path was still most difficult.

* * *

In 1937 Western Samoans saw their first aeroplane since the seaplane off the cruiser *Dunedin* in 1930. A single seater DH53 *Moth* with a Bristol *Cherub* engine was unloaded from the *Wairuna* on June 10. The owner was Lance Corporal J. M. H. Bower, District Commissioner at Aleipata. Bower had only recently arrived back in Apia from a visit to New Zealand where he acquired his pilot's licence and an airworthiness certificate for the *Moth*.

The aircraft was formerly owned by the Civil Aviation Department in Australia who had sold it to the Aero Club of New South Wales. They in turn disposed of the plane to Bower.

Peter Paul, a German pioneer arrived in Apia in 1881. He constructed many buildings in and around Apia. Paul died on January 1, 1938, aged 88, and had lived in Samoa for 56 years. During that time he was the originator of the Paul clan so well known and respected in Western Samoa. Paul had earlier been an engineer in Hawaii. He went to Fiji to build their first sugar mill, later constructing trading posts in Tonga for the German traders DH & PG.

Not everyone was satisfied with the *Mau* aims, as the much criticised 1936 "Goodwill Mission" had yet to prove beneficial. Indeed most planters had been placed in an embarrassing position when the Chinese labourers were repatriated.

Obtaining a local work force had proved impossible as the planters had always maintained. Labourers from Niue had been brought to Apia but though they worked harder than Samoans the move was not successful.

The Samoan Government was said by some to be closely linked with the Nelson-controlled *Mau*. With O.F. directing the rejuvenated *Mau* many of the group insisted on interfering in government affairs about which they understood very little.

For a while the Administration was a puppet in the control of the *Mau* movement. Gradually the New Zealand Government in Wellington changed their attitude to Apia rejecting many demands from the Samoans.

But the situation was not made easier for the Europeans after NZ Labour Minister Langston stated that the prestige of whites was regarded too highly in Samoa.

* * *

Mary Croudace took a lease of the Casino Hotel early in 1939 following many requests from local residents. She realised the end was near for her husband who was suffering from cancer. He died in April, 1940, when their only child, Jean, was nearly twenty.

Robert Douglas Croudace came to Samoa as a boy

and after being educated in Australia he commenced in the accounting profession in Apia. In addition to working for John Rothschild and Company he was also associated with the Samoan Public Service, Gold Star Transport Company, and G. T. Jackson. He was elected a member of the Legislative Council in 1920 and served for a number of years. At various times he was president of the Apia Chamber of Commerce and the British Club.

Ever since the death of High Chief Tamasese during the *Mau* procession in 1929 there had been an annual pilgrimage to his grave at Lepea. On the ninth anniversary mourners were headed by the Pesega band followed by *Mau* guards and then about 300 women led by Masiofo Tamasese. O. F. Nelson and his daughters joined the half-mile long procession.

*   *   *

On March 20, 1939, High Chief Faumuina Fiame, then inspector of Samoan Police, was awarded the title of Mata'afa, the former Royal Family of Samoa.

"There were so many problems in those early days and I just didn't know what the Administration would do next," Aggie explained. "The authorities seemed intent on preventing me establishing the boarding house on a standard that would encourage tourism. At least that's the way it appeared to me at the time."

Aggie thought that now she had mellowed a little, maybe her criticism of the Administration was a little harsh.

"I recall one incident just after I was able to get a licence to operate," she recounted smiling. "The Administrator decided maybe he should raid the premises."

Her son Alan had just been born and she was feeding the baby.

"The Administration had cut off the electricity because there just wasn't any money to pay the account," said Aggie. "Times were so hard, and I was almost in the depths of despair when the soldiers arrived in force to carry out the raid.

"At least the Administrator, who was there in person, had the decency to withdraw his troops. Next day he sent a letter apologising for staging a raid at such a time as baby Alan's feeding time."

Doctor Monoghan was the Government officer with whom Aggie had regular consultations concerning the issue of points for liquor supplies. On one occasion he refused her request when she reported sick. Aggie was in urgent need of a bottle of gin for an important function and spirits were quite scarce at the time.

The doctor said, "You should know that everyone is advised to keep a certain amount of liquor in readiness for any illness or emergency that might occur."

"I have a bad pain in my side," Aggie remonstrated, "and feel very sick. I would like some extra points."

When the doctor told Aggie he would issue a prescription for medicine but it would not include alcohol, Aggie was furious and told the officer exactly what she thought of him and his decision. Colonial doctors with authority in those days were not used to this sort of candour from the locals. They usually had a means of retaliation to impose on any who offended their dignity.

The doctor reported to the Administration that Aggie might have to prepare sly grog as it seemed she did not have sufficient points to buy liquor for a special party.

"Certainly at that particular time," laughed Aggie, "I wasn't involved in sly grog, I was able to borrow a bottle of gin from a friend. So our party was a success after all."

The points system for liquor went right back to the days of the mandate given to New Zealand by the League of Nations after the end of World War I.

Aggie explains: "In the German times there was a positive distinction between Europeans and Samoans. There was a wide selection of different beers, wines and spirits available from several hotels — but only for Europeans. The Samoans were not permitted to drink liquor and the penalties for possession were severe.

"When the New Zealand Government passed the law making Western Samoa a dry country they were carrying out a direction from the League of Nations that the supply of liquor to 'natives' was to be prohibited."

And in their haste the New Zealand parliamentarians did not give any thought to the Europeans based in Samoa. The whole country was to be dry — Europeans and "natives" alike!

The government statute only permitted liquor to be imported into Western Samoa for medicinal, sacramental, or industrial purposes.

"Yes," continued Aggie, who probably knew more about the points system than most people, "the Europeans thought that the 'medicinal use' was a way around the regulations without creating a great protest about prohibition.

"The Chief Medical Officer was authorised to issue permits as a matter of course to all Europeans. The system was really a complete farce because the number of points issued to each person had nothing to do with their health. It was only their social status or the wages they earned that governed the distinction.

"The points system was a monthly affair and at the end of each month any unused points were cancelled. The scale of points allocated by the medical officers varied from 24 a month for a single person up to 108 for a top-ranking administrative officer."

When the United Nations took over from the League of Nations the prohibition laws could have been relaxed immediately but NZ did not do so. Various committees were appointed to make recommendations, but even by 1960 little had changed.

"One thing did change a little," Aggie said, "and this was the allocation of points to Samoans. Those of high standing and good reputation were awarded monthly quotas, and gradually the number of these people increased. Visitors to Samoa could go to the police station and obtain a ration for a stay of only a week or two.

"This visitor quota helped me a lot in the running of the hotel because every guest would turn over his points to me. The greatest help was the non-drinker — his points were like diamonds."

I asked Aggie did she have any special secrets in getting black-market points in those prohibition days.

"Yes, of course I did, but I'm not saying anything about that," answered Aggie with a twinkle in her eye, "because you never know, they might bring that prohibition system in again one day, and I'll be ready for them."

It's hardly likely now despite PM Mata'afa's controversial 1968 statement advocating total prohibition in Western Samoa. The country now has its own brewery, acquired at considerable expense from West Germany.

First mooted early in 1976 the brewery is operated jointly by the Goverment and a firm of German brewers. Opened in November, 1978, the trade name of the beer is Vailima— the same as Stevenson's original home which is now Government House.

Early in 1939 things looked serious for some of the Germans in Apia when the local branch of the Nazi party was ordered to be disbanded by an instruction from the German Consul-General in Wellington. The group's activities had been subject to criticism by the British residents and even many of the German citizens disapproved of their actions. Like most other similar banned bodies throughout the world the members no doubt went underground.

Seldom in trouble no matter what country, it was surprising that 34 Chinese migrants were arraigned before the High Court in Apia on June 21, 1939.

Surprising also that the unfortunates were bracketed with 34 Samoan women — all accused of cohabitating. The law said that Samoan women must not live with Chinese coolies on European plantations.

Most of the women had small children, proving they had cohabitated for some time. They were each given three days' imprisonment. Upon release they were ordered back to their villages where the chiefs were responsible to see that the ladies did not return to the Chinese who were said "to treat their Samoan wives kindly and generously."

The New Zealand authorities were determined to stop the "illicit" association despite the fact that the children of a Polynesian-Chinese union are very good lookers and particularly industrious.

Tourists continued to arrive in Western Samoa during wartime but there was only a trickle. Students went to New Zealand to complete their studies but here again only on a limited scale.

In October, 1941, the Western Samoa Mail reported that Reginald Phillips, nephew of Mr. & Mrs. E. F. Paul, had again become heavyweight boxing champion at the Sacred Heart College in NZ.

Many haunts for explorers in Samoa have long been forgotten although their mention to Aggie will quickly spark an interesting story.

"It was about 1941," recalled Aggie, "that a Charles Reed was wandering around the bush near Lake Lanuto'o.

"This man was a nature lover and had told us of his studies of the flying foxes. In addition to the well known fruit eating bat there are two smaller insect feeding bats, which live in caves near the shores.

"If only people would explore many inland parts of Samoa they would discover such things as the nest of the small bats which have a body about the size of a mouse," continued Aggie.

"These bats build nests like a circular tobacco pouch with an entrance hole less than two inches in diameter. The whole nest is only about the size of a man's hand and is covered with a secreted cemented moss. There are some exciting caves not far from Lake Lanuto'o where Reed told us he trudged knee deep through pure bat guano— an exploration that led him nearly two miles from the entrance of the cave."

*   *   *

When the Japanese attacked Pearl Harbor on December 7, 1941, the New Zealand authorities on December 10 declared a state of emergency for Western Samoa.

The official report advised that "the people should not be in any way alarmed but as far as possible those who do not have business in Apia and do not require to reside in this area should go to the outside districts."

The residents of Apia did not take too kindly to this invitation to evacuate to the bush, particularly as there appeared to be little likelihood that town properties could be adequately safeguarded during their absence.

The Government warned that "all bright lights to be extinguished or dimmed, particularly those visible from the sea. Co-operate otherwise a strict blackout may be enforced. All unessential travel by bus or taxi must cease. Rationing of benzine, flour and bread is to operate. Public should not take a pessimistic view of things", concluded the bulletin.

Western Samoa was now really on a wartime footing for the first time.

Aggie's husband, Charlie, was assisting in the raising of war relief funds and was honorary secretary of the race meeting committee. Grey was a keen member of the Samoa Defence Force, a group which, like many others in the British Commonwealth, was hopelessly short of even elementary equipment.

The initial Administration bulletin was soon followed by a still more dramatic instruction which read:—

"In the event of air raid sirens will be blown, but warning may not be possible. Take cover at once, leave buildings, lie down in deep ditches, etc. Everyone should prepare a dugout or similar cover.

"In the event of a raid by a surface party or landing party four tolls will be rung on the Catholic Cathedral, plus similar repeats in other churches. Wooden drums and conches should repeat the four distinct tolls, carrying it from village to village throughout the country.

"Leave your home and take food, clothing, knives

and an axe, hurricane lantern, kerosene, cooking utensils — get them together now! Hide or bury your valuable things, turn loose any animals. Use pack horses if you have them and go inland. Build yourself a brush house, stay quiet. Travel by bush tracks not on the roads; keep out of sight of planes.

"Special police can be identified by: Europeans — wearing tin hats or a felt hat and wearing a belt and revolver; Samoans — white towel around the neck."

"It seemed that Western Samoa would be closely involved with the war," explained Aggie. "With America and Japan fighting in the Pacific and American Samoa only a few miles away, we all realised our lives would change. But how greatly and in what way we didn't know. Thinking back perhaps it is just as well we didn't know."

Chapter 9
Pearl Harbor and Apia (1942-1945)

War in the Pacific which followed the Japanese bombing of Pearl Harbor on December 7. 1941, certainly did have a profound effect on life in Western Samoa. Although the country was already on a war time footing there was little possibility of any real enemy action until the Japanese participation.

In 1939 Western Samoa was automatically involved in the European war because of its designation as a New Zealand trustee territory by the League of Nations ruling at the Peace Conference following World War I.

Following the US entry into the war it was inevitable that American forces would soon occupy Western Samoa as part of their planned strategy throughout the Pacific.

The Japanese held the initiative and were wreaking havoc as they moved with lightning speed in Asia and the South Pacific.

Before the Americans were able to do anything about Western Samoa the Japanese brought the war to the doorsteps of the Polynesians. Early on Sunday morning January 11, a submarine sneaked along the northern coast of American Samoa and bombarded Pago Pago with 5.9 inch shells. Although some shots fell into the harbor generally the marksmanship was good.

No-one was killed during the raid and only three persons were wounded, but the incident did provoke some immediate action by Washington. Pago Pago saw military activity previously unknown in the forty years since it became a US naval base after the 1899 Treaty. Troops, supplies, medical and hospital facilities appeared in short time.

But despite the frenzied happenings in Pago it appeared nothing was being done for the protection of Western Samoa. Many locals began to think they were being left to the mercy of a Japanese invasion. Nauru and Ocean Island had been occupied by the enemy and things looked grim for the allies.

During February, 1942, a Grumman seaplane brought two high-ranking US Marine Corps officers to Apia. "We thought," Aggie told me, "that this was the beginning of the US occupation, but it was not the case. We were most disillusioned to learn later that the officers were making a survey of possible localities on Upolu where the Japanese might construct airfields if they invaded our island."

News of the reason for the visit of the Grumman possibly had a depressing effect on the morale of the Western Samoa Defence Force, a stout-hearted band of locals, and it could have been the straw that broke the camel's back. Because not long afterwards a request was made to the Administration to disband the force.

Their reasoning was logical. They were all loyal Samoans but what resistance could they offer to the Japanese? Any opposition would, in their opinion, greatly increase the risk of danger to the Samoan people.

Impatient for aid, Western Samoa did not have long to wait for action. On March 24 the US *Swan*, a minesweeper, made a hurried visit to Apia to discharge an advance party of about one hundred Marines and Seebees on to the Beach. Of course this was just a beginning, and no Samoan could have realised exactly what an impact such an occupation would have on the daily lives of the people.

Three days later on March 27, the *President Garfield* and a number of other huge transports eased their way into Apia Harbor. Many thousands of US Marines were disembarked. But even these were only the forerunners of the major occupying forces still to arrive.

The activity on the Beach continued. The army traffic was intense. Because the small wharfs could not handle the volume of lightering needed from the ships in the harbor, LST and other craft deposited their loads on various spots along the seafront, including a spot right opposite Aggie's.

Construction of the airfield soon began on the present site of Faleolo airport. Guns, tanks, and bulldozers were everywhere.

When America entered the war Aggie Grey was in the midst of one of the most depressing times of her life. Her husband was bankrupt, and it looked as though they would lose their charming home to satisfy the creditors.

Although Aggie had earlier lived a more-or-less carefree life she did not shirk the challenge now confronting her future. The indifferent health of her husband, lack of money, the responsibilities of rearing her family, were some of the major problems she faced.

To add to this profound misery news came to Aggie that her daughter Pele was seriously ill in Pago. Aggie recalled: "Things were so bad I had to borrow money to go by boat to Pago. Pele had typhoid fever and was very sick. I stayed with her for several months in Pago and brought her back to health.

"Some people believe that I opened a boarding house in Pago but that is not true. I had my hands full looking after Pele. It was a worrying time because I knew the problems in Apia would just not right themselves automatically. I would soon need to return there, and hoped for the best."

When Aggie returned to Apia her Swann pioneering spirit was put to test. She battled for some solution that would lift her family out of a seemingly hopeless situation.

I asked Aggie what were her thoughts in those days — did she ever regret that she married Gordon Hay MacKenzie when by accepting any one of many proposals of marriage from rich traders of Western Samoa she could have had a reasonably assured life of luxury?

Without hesitation Aggie replied that she met Gordon, fell in love with him, and was married at the age of twenty. "There were many seeking my hand in Apia in those days," Aggie said, "I liked most of them but it was Gordon I fell in love with and never regretted my decision to marry him."

At the time of the US occupation Mary had the lease of the Casino. She was doing very well, especially after the old German DH & PG building was taken over for use as an American officers quarters. Mary, who had an excellent reputation both as a gourmet chef and as a manager, was asked to continue in her executive position.

American dollars were flowing freely in Apia, and the wealth of equipment landed by the Marines was an eye-opener to the Samoans. The mythical *papalagi* ships from the Pacific heavens had really come to Polynesia.

With their South Seas communistic views that all good things should be shared, the Samoans quickly found ways to acquire tyres, fuel, batteries, cigarettes, and other luxuries on the very best trading terms.

The Swann girls were always a closely knit group when it came to troubles in the *aiga*. With her experience at the Casino, Mary could see great possibilities for a genuine eating house, a snack bar, call it what you wish, in the American-occupied Apia of 1942.

Perhaps this was the opportunity that Aggie was looking for, a chance to make some quick money no matter if it meant hard work.

With Mary's advice and urging, Aggie began selling hamburgers and coffee in March, 1942. Aggie's Store next to her present day hotel was the chosen location. Here, where her father's pharmacy had flourished, Aggie got her big break.

After some months passed Aggie decided that food sales might well be the golden opportunity she needed to establish a new business. And so it was hamburgers and coffee for a quarter that got Aggie off to a grand start. The demand was positively phenomenal.

There was only one "town" in Western Samoa and even though there were several makeshift restaurants in Apia, usually they were tagged "off bounds" by the American health authorities — but not Aggie's.

They sold thousands of the home-made delicacies, just what the lonely enlisted men were needing, a touch of main street right in the centre of the Pacific. Not only did Aggie have the respect and the friendship of the ordinary Marine but the officers also flocked to the weatherboard building down by the mouth of the Vaisigano River.

Aggie and her *aiga* worked the long hours necessary to make a success of the hamburger store, locating good meat, the best of baked bread, even salt and pepper were sometimes in short supply.

During these busy days Aggie had no time to worry about extensions and improvements to her next door Club. These could all come later. Aggie's Hotel of today had already made its debut as a Club in the reconstructed and historic International Hotel, the hostelry with a past going back to the swashbuckling days of Bully Hayes. But it was really the success of the hamburgers and coffee that made it all possible.

Aggie was happy with the successful beginning, although there had been many frustrating problems. "There were always the difficulties of supplies," she told me. "We were faced with accepting good fresh meat without worrying where it came from — no questions asked. Sometimes we would trade handicrafts to the cooks on a ship. In return we would get provisions — meat, ketchup, mustard, and other condiments we needed for the hamburger store."

After the hamburger enterprise had launched Aggie into the business world she had to think of other ways to consolidate while the Americans were still in occupation.

I wondered how the knowledge of the past history of her present building effected Aggie. Did she ever think about the rollicking days of the International Hotel, or the unhappy period when the New Zealand police occupied the building during the *Mau* troubles, or perhaps the wilder times of the British Club?

"These things never worried me," Aggie explained. "We had lived opposite the old International Hotel when it was near where the RSA Club now stands. There were wild get-togethers and drinking parties in those days so that the noise was terrific some nights. But I got used to these happenings like the rest of the family. And when you think of them today, well nothing seems quite as bad as it appeared to us in those days when we were young."

Charlie Grey came to Apia to manage the firm of S. H. Meredith (Samoa) Ltd. The business was in financial difficulties and Grey was unable to bring it back to a workable basis despite several promising periods when it appeared that they may have turned the corner.

After the firm closed Grey went to work for Peter Fabricius and Maggie. Things had not gone well for Charlie and he was bankrupt. This meant losing their beautiful home on Vailima Road and the property was bought by Geoff Jackson, an Apia solicitor.

When Charlie Grey died on November 26, 1943, Aggie was faced with the task of establishing her small business so that she could bring up her family in the standards to which the Swann *aiga* had been accustomed.

There are countless stories to be told of amusing and many serious incidents during the US occupation days. There is an incident concerning the captain of a ship called the *Admiral Wiley* that was unloading in Apia. During the tight security it was not permissible for any small craft to approach a ship in the harbor at night. The vessel was anchored just opposite Aggie's. The captain had spent a day ashore and had indulged in considerable quantities of bush gin until he reached the stage where he was barely capable of conducting himself in any normal manner.

Darkness had approached and the captain wished to return to his ship but the only possible transport was a Samoan *paopao*. As he approached the ship in the canoe he was challenged by the watchman, a marine who could not believe that this unkempt character was the captain. Finally, after considerable argument he convinced the guard, went aboard, and into his cabin.

Extremely annoyed at the treatment he had received on his own ship, and befuddled with bush gin, he burst out of his cabin with pistols flaming. The guard had no alternative but to shoot him down.

He was buried in Apia, a lesson to all who indulged in bush gin to excess.

The *Admiral Wiley* was left without a skipper so the first mate took charge but had no hope of getting the ship out of the harbor. He was rated as a chief officer, but it appears his prewar trade was that of haberdashery. He had undergone a crash course in the merchant navy to take command of ships.

Obviously he was incapable of taking the ship to sea so the *Admiral Wiley* had to await the arrival of a competent skipper from overseas. During this enforced stay reports say that none of the crew members on shore leave ever touched a drop of bush gin!

Another story concerns an Apia trader, Emilio, during the early days of the American wartime garrisoning at Pago Pago. Always it was a better proposition for the merchants to ship fresh vegetables to American Samoa where they would obtain much better prices than in Apia.

The MV *Samoa* carrying a full cargo of produce from Emilio sailed from Apia Harbour while the likeable amigo was enjoying himself sipping a whisky at a waterfront bar.

When he discovered the ship had sailed without him there was considerable panic, but it was also a time for quick decisions. Equipped with a pistol, Emilio boarded the MV *Taumatai* anchored in the harbour. At gun point, like a Mexican pirate, he forced the captain to set sail for Pago, aiming to overtake the *Samoa*.

Emilio knew he would have to reach Pago before the ship otherwise his produce would be quickly sold, although he would not see the money. At a point halfway to Tutuila, the *Taumatai* caught up with the *Samoa*. Emilio boarded the *Samoa* and continued to Pago guarding his cargo.

He must have realised there would be some trouble when he returned to Apia so he delayed his departure from American Samoa for about a month. During this time he hoped that tempers might cool and the incident forgotten.

When he finally returned Emilio found to his dismay the New Zealand administration was having the unfortunate amigo charged with armed robbery, quite a serious offence during wartime.

Despite all protestations Emilio was found guilty and went to gaol. Various pleas on his behalf secured an early release with the substitution of a fine. Evidence was given that he had been a most patriotic worker for his country. To the authorities Emilio gave a sincere promise never to repeat the offence.

Emilio's familiar face is no longer seen down by the harbour lights in Beach Road. This lovable and friendly character died in 1978.

Gone is another oldtimer from the groups who regularly gather at sunset to enjoy a quiet drink.

American officers used to park their jeeps in front of Aggie Grey's, go in for a few drinks and maybe stay a little longer than they had first intended. Frequently it is recorded that during their relaxation in the hotel some persons unknown had bodily supported the chassis of the vehicles so as to quickly remove all four wheels and completely drain the petrol tanks.

Easily imagined is the consternation of the American officers as they clambered into their jeeps to return to barracks often to find that the only transportation they had left was a body, chassis, and steering wheel. Sometimes parts of the motors were stealthily removed because such things as batteries and spark plugs were easily disposed of in those days of shortages.

Very soon regular details of American Military Police were found to be closely guarding all vehicles parked out the front of Aggie's.

During the occupation American officers were mostly able to obtain a reasonable supply of beer and spirits. With the GIs it was a different matter. Often their rations were issued out at most irregular intervals. These deprived Americans would buy as much illicit liquor that could be stilled, even specially treated coconut juice. Anything that could be fermented was turned into an alcoholic beverage. Raisins, currants, rice, and corn were some of the ingredients that went towards producing that favourite brew, bush gin, which usually sold at $2 a bottle.

Situated on the top floor of Aggie's there was a large still, capably managed by a well-known resident. This home-made equipment was reputed to have turned out an excellent brew, although not sufficiently strong to turn the drinker blind—like the wood alcohol in Manila.

A 7 p.m. curfew was imposed in Apia and other areas of Upolu requiring everybody to be off the streets at that hour. But this restriction did not prevent the marketing of bush gin.

Although a completely unsophisticated brew compared with still liquor, an age-old island recipe produced palm toddy, a popular prohibition drink in Samoa. Often the "toddytappers" had to shin more than thirty feet up notched tree trunks to harvest the liquor supply.

Tapping toddy was simple and effective. Coconut

buds were selected by the climber, cut into with a knife and bound tightly with palm fronds. Glass jam jars were hung below the selected buds so that the toddy juice slowly dripped into the containers. Resembling barley water in appearance, the non-alcoholic liquid with a fizzy tang when fresh, was guaranteed to produce raucous laughter and revelry followed by mild intoxication and a slight hangover.

*   *   *

In 1945, GI occupation-boredom had become a problem in Pago Pago, as indeed it had in most of the South West Pacific war zone.

Aggie was then catering, in fact was specialising in the needs of these homesick Americans. Many were thoroughly tired of a monotonous diet of chilli con carne and pork loaf. They yearned for the homely conditions, the welcome that they knew would await them in Apia.

About this time James A. Michener was serving his time for Uncle Sam as a naval historical officer with special assignments in the eastern Pacific.

Over the years *Tales of the South Pacific*, with its famous character Bloody Mary, has caused Aggie considerable pain and sadness. It all began when Willard Price in his *Adventures in Paradise* hinted a connection existed between the Tonkinese leading lady and Aggie Grey. Some columnists were quick to amplify the writer's comment.

As the story circulated it became so exaggerated that newspapers claimed Aggie was most certainly the prototype of Bloody Mary.

Some years ago on a visit to Australia she was billed with embarrassing headlines about this association. Aggie was so upset with the allegations that she drastically curtailed her visit and returned to Apia.

From that time onward Aggie has carefully concealed her distrust of journalists. Many have been politely but coldly received; many just left Samoa after unsuccessful interview attempts.

This treatment of journalists has been a difficult decision for Aggie who knows full well that publicity and tourism go hand in hand. Short story and feature writers have long relied on the Bloody Mary inference to get editorial acceptance.

On one occasion the widely-read Sydney-based *Pacific Islands Monthly* published comment that Aggie represented only the good parts of the Tonkinese madam, not the bad.

Stories with such a salacious flavour are not easily quashed. They often persist in spite of vehement denials by the principals involved.

James A. Michener had really said very little about the controversy, so I felt that if he could be prevailed upon then Aggie's biography must include the famous writer's personal views.

Michener told me that early in 1945 the manuscript of *Tales of the South Pacific* was already in the offices of the Macmillan Company in New York.

"It was after this that I was often stationed in American Samoa," he said. "And it was unutterably dull and militarily stuffy.

"A naval man was considered reasonably intelligent if he could wangle, under any pretext whatever, a trip to British Samoa where he could go to Aggie Grey's Hotel, eat some decent food, get some good Australian beer, and listen to the wild stories Aggie told."

Thinking back the thirty years was not a problem for Michener and it goes to prove how indelible were his impressions of these happy excursions.

"I managed to reach Apia half a dozen times," he

explained, "always with a gasp of relief and a cry of joy at seeing dear Aggie again. She was ebullient, effervescent, outrageous, illegal, and terribly bright. She and her crew must have bilked the American forces out of a couple of million dollars worth of services, and never was wartime money better spent."

To be an outstanding business success in Samoa it is important to be a good manipulator and be able to make a quick and correct decision. Such a judgment will benefit not only the skilful operator, but provide direct gain, even if marginal, to as many of the *aiga* as possible. This way the family is anxious to participate and will aid with constructive advice hoping to make an approved project a certain success.

It was no surprise to me when Michener asserted: "The catalogue of Aggie's manipulations would fill a small book, of her kindness a library."

And in the accepted way of life in Samoa, to be classified as a smart manipulator is really praise indeed. In short, successful business in Apia is negotiated by clever manipulators.

Michener continued, "I loved her. She was unfailingly generous, robust, and instructive. When I returned to New York to edit the manuscript of my first book and I needed a reference point as to what Bloody Mary would do or say, I simply recalled Aggie and had my answer."

Tales of the South Pacific launched Michener on the road to fame as a writer. Since then he has certainly become one of the most successful *tusitala* of this century.

For me, a small-time columnist and author, to question the famed writer could be considered complete and utter effrontery. Yet I've always believed that much remained unexplained about the Bloody

Mary fantasy and I was hopeful Michener would tell me the true history.

He needed no encouragement. He emphasised: "Aggie was not the prototype Bloody Mary. That worthy Tonkinese was on paper long before I met Aggie. But it was Aggie, and she alone, who fortified my writing in the editing stage, who remained as the visualisation of the island manipulator when the play was in formation, and who lives, in a curious way, as the real-life Bloody Mary."

On a happy note, James Michener, who had cleared Aggie of the many unpleasant newspaper inferences, concluded: "She was a marvellous woman, inventive and a creation of the war. I still love her."

Obviously then some indirect credit must go to Aggie for the completeness of *Tales of the South Pacific*. She may have played an important role in the success of the book, but it seems Aggie was definitely not Bloody Mary.

When I told Aggie of Michener's comments she was quite elated, as though a heavy weight had been lifted from her shoulders.

"I remember him clearly," she said, describing how Michener always sat in his favourite seat at the corner of the bar.

"We generally got advance news of his visits, always with specific orders for the best of steak and eggs. Those boys had huge appetites. It was almost as if they were starved in Pago," laughed Aggie.

"Michener was a quiet well-behaved one, didn't talk very much but I had a feeling he absorbed everything he heard in our bar. Certainly he must have listened to my South Sea ramblings."

As 1945 wore on, the Americans began evacuating in a steady stream, heading for the new theatres of war in the North West Pacific, thence to the

Philippines, and finally on to Japan. And when peace came to the South Seas the occupation forces were soon away from Western Samoa. The flood of freely-spent dollars was ending but the GIs left in their wake many well-established Apia businesses.

Aggie's Hotel was one of them, but it was necessary for Aggie to consolidate. Years of hard work lay ahead of her before she could sit back and relax in the knowledge that her ambitions were fulfilled — before she became mine host of the most popular hotel in the South Pacific.

*   *   *

Most Samoans believe in the ghosts of their ancestors, but generally this belief is confined to their own villages.

When staying in New York I asked a high chief did he believe in ghosts. "Yes," he replied, "but not here in New York. But in my village there are surely the ghosts of my ancestors."

There are many spirit stories to be told by the older *tusitala* of Samoa, both by men and women. Chapters could be written on the escapades of these frequenters of the "underworld."

My good friend, Eddie Stehlin, O.B.E., has told me many tales of Samoan mythology, stories that defy challenge by the *papalagi*, however incredible they may seem.

One day he asked me had I heard the story of the enchanted wall of Savai'i. I had known about it but as Eddie's experiences were firsthand and personal I told him I was eager to hear his version.

"At the very western tip of Savai'i," he began, "there is a point on the coastline which the Samoans refer to as the *Fafa O Sauali'i*.

118

"*Fafa* means endless chasm, *O* stands for of, and *sauali'i* is another name for demons, in this case — the elite of the demons! There are two large crevices in the rocks at the same point. One crevice the Samoans say is the road of the spirits to the island of Upolu; the other crevice is the pathway of the spirits to the island of Savai'i.

"From this point the enchanted wall of Samoa begins and crosses the island of Savai'i over the mountains and hills to emerge at the north coast at a point called Tuasivi, which means the ridge or backbone.

"I can recall two incidents connected with the wall for which I can vouch. Several years ago an American by the name of Flaherty came to Samoa to make a film which was titled 'Moana of the South Seas.' This is the same man who filmed 'Nanook of the North.'

"In his search for suitable scenes to film, Flaherty went as far as the village of Tufutofoe which lies east of the enchanted stone wall. Unfortunately Flaherty became ill in Tufutofoe; he was so sick that the Government steamer *Lady Roberts* was required to take him to the Apia hospital. As there was no reef passage in Tufutofoe through which the people could take Flaherty out to the boat, he had to be carried overland to the village of Falealupo which lies west of the wall.

"In other words," Eddie emphasised, "the patient had to be taken over the wall, from Tufutofoe to Falealupo. The Samoans believe that any sick person who has to be carried across this wall will certainly die. No matter how sick you are, if you can walk across and over the wall you will be all right, but if you must be carried across, the end will be sure."

On the day they carried Flaherty across the wall it seems there was considerable speculation by the

Samoans as to what to do with their European patient. The Samoans think for some reason the evil spells of certain of their demons are effective only on themselves but not on the *papalagi*.

Flaherty, the story goes, was not made to walk but was carefully carried across the wall.

Eddie believes that because of this confrontation with the spirits many Samoans, despite their beliefs, did not think Flaherty would live.

However he was soon safely aboard the *Lady Roberts* at Falealupo en route to Apia where he recovered in hospital. In due course he completed the filming of "Moana of the South Seas" and returned to America. Perhaps Flaherty was rather lucky that anti-*papalagi* demons were not on duty at the time he crossed the wall.

"The other incident involved my own family," continued Eddie. "Our first child was due to arrive and I had left my wife with her parents, who were Methodist missionaries, at Asau. We had to cross the wall to return to where we were living in Savai'i at that time.

"The Samoans believe that a pregnant woman must not cross the wall immediately but must go up to it three times, and then she may cross with safety. They are firmly convinced that if this is not done the unborn child will surely die.

"When we got up to the wall with our two carriers and our luggage, we halted so as to hold council with all concerned as to what was the proper thing to do. Must my wife go up to the wall three times before crossing or should we disregard the superstitions of our people and continue on our way?

"Although personally I did not attach much significance to the superstition, I was somewhat afraid for the safety of my wife and our firstborn. I decided

120

to take no chances — I made her walk up to the wall three times, very much to her disgust, and then the whole party went across. To the present day my wife still enjoys good health and so does our firstborn, a daughter."

I asked Aggie did she believe in ghosts. She answered "No," but after some thought she recalled an occasion when she felt the supernatural was close at hand.

This was late one afternoon when, together with a girl friend, Aggie went "shelling" — the collecting of shell fish amongst the rocks in shallow water.

It was a close, humid, thundery day with dark clouds hiding the sun and flashes of lightning stabbing the sky.

"Everything suddenly seemed very quiet," Aggie said as she described the scene, "so quiet we could barely hear the breakers on the reef.

"Walking amongst the rocks I sensed that someone was pushing me. When I looked around there was nobody. Calling excitedly to my friend who was some yards ahead of me, I told her about the sensations.

"My friend advised me to move up out of the water completely, and see if the effect was the same when on land. I did this and experienced no further feeling of the supernatural, if this is what it was."

Aggie went on to say that she considered that if Samoans were good Christians they should not believe in ghosts as their faith in God should surmount any thoughts they might have of the spirit underworld.

However, to be on the safe side, it is a common belief amongst Samoans that it is a good idea to be friendly with the ghosts of the old days as well as the new gods of the missionaries.

Chapter 10

Peace in the Pacific (1946-1954)

New Year's Eve was celebrated in Apia in a manner befitting the heralding of the first year of peace following the end of World War II.

Aggie realised that for her the years ahead would be a tremendous struggle to exist, to earn a living. The Americans had gone and with them the big spending money. To be sure, there were hoards of GI dollars in the shops and clubs of Apia. Samoa was no different to any other country occupied by the Americans.

Some chose to sit back and enjoy their earnings, to watch them fritter away, not caring about the future. Aggie did not think this way at all. She wanted to build up her business from the wartime foundations. She had a family to keep and money was getting more difficult as the New Zealand administration tightened the liquor laws.

"When I think back," Aggie told me, "those laws were really laughable the way they operated and the way they were explained to the Samoans. Officially Western Samoa was still a prohibition country but a permit to buy alcohol was granted to any adult European who applied for one.

"Strictly speaking, the more money they earned the 'unhealthier' they were classed, because they were given extra points to buy 'medicinal' liquor."

And it was a really remarkable system. To devise such a racially discriminatory arrangement today would be unthinkable.

Towards the end of 1946 the United Nations began their sessions on the fate of countries that had been mandated territories under the League of Nations. The future of Western Samoa was now to be decided in New York with very little regard to that nation's wishes, certainly none at all at that early stage.

A group of people representing mainly Western countries had formed into several groups. Their task at UN was initially to discuss the fate of "dependent people" — apparently meaning those not able or not capable of looking after themselves.

This committee seems to have separated into two groups — one concerned with the future of the colonial regimes and the other studying the trusteeship questions. The representatives in each body no doubt followed closely the dictates and briefing of the governments to whom they belonged.

As there were no trusteeships at that stage there could be no Trusteeship Council. When the first was appointed then the council could become operative so there was an apparent eagerness to launch the first nation into the "guidance" or "captivity" of an allied country of distinction.

There were draft agreements to be considered for British Tanganyika, Belgian Ruanda-Urindi, Australian New Guinea, British Togoland, French Togoland, and Western Samoa.

All had been pre-World War "mandated territories" and the aggregate population was over 15 million. Of this total Western Samoa had only 100,000.

None was anxious to be the first to have their future decided so it fell to Samoa, with the smallest population and maybe the least problems, to head the agenda list for initial discussions.

On December 13, 1946, the Trusteeship Council became an accomplished fact. Western Samoa was a trust territory of New Zealand and the Kiwi delegates now had the job of telling the Polynesian people the result.

That the Samoans were not told in advance of the plans undoubtedly saved the New Zealanders at UN from the complications of counter-proposals and undoubtedly pleas for a much greater say in government, if not self-government. In fairness to New Zealand, the Administration in Apia at least did keep the nation informed of the various stages of development as they were occurring at UN.

Of course this was too late for any direct action from the Samoans. The general reaction in Apia was that it was perhaps a step forward from their previous mandated status. However their goal of independence did not really seem any closer.

When the trustee territory was approved in July, 1947, there began the first of many visits by teams from UN to Apia to view the situation and report back to New York.

And so the situation at the end of 1947 was that the Samoan leaders agreed that the plans for their eventual independence were firmly established, only the actual date was obscure.

"The change to trusteeship did not alter conditions very much for us," Aggie told me. "The New Zealanders were still in charge and we resumed work and business with regulations much the same as before the war."

* * *

Every Pacific island port seems to have boasted a local photographer of renown. Apia had "Old Tat" who must have known everyone of any importance in Samoa. Tattersall came to Apia at the age of sixteen as a photographer's assistant. He worked for J. Davis who died in 1893.

"Of course I knew Old Tat very well," Aggie told me. "His little studio on the Beach was a popular place with Samoans. He married a Samoan girl. Tat came to Apia from Auckland in 1886. He told me he knew Robert Louis Stevenson intimately."

Tattersall certainly remembered *Tusitala* well for he had taken many photographs at Vailima. He told Aggie everyone liked Mr. Stevenson who was always so obliging and good-humoured even when he was ill.

"Yes, Tat was a hard worker," recalled Aggie. "They built themselves a shuttered house and had a nice garden with mango trees, tropical gardens and even a grass tennis court.

"Tat had photographs of the Apia hurricane in 1889. This storm stayed one of his most vivid memories. I think his lifetime collection of photographs must have been one of the most remarkable in the whole Pacific."

These unique records of early days of Western Samoa have gradually disappeared. The photos of the molten lava flows on Savai'i, the denuded coconut trees, irreplaceable on-the-spot shots which Old Tat risked his life to take, are no more. The remaining negatives from his collection were destroyed during the 1966 hurricane.

In 1950 Alfred John Tattersall died in Apia— a remarkable gentleman more than 80 years of age.

*   *   *

Tourist parties who are taken to Lefaga Beach are told that this was the site of the film "Return to Paradise", and the tour leaders happily enlighten the visitors that it was the famous American filmstar Gary Cooper who played the lead in the movie.

The film was made in 1952, and was based on a story by James Michener. Tourists from the US, Germany, Italy, Japan and all parts of the world have been shown the featured beach. The guide chatter will continue to be interesting for a few more years, but just how long? In another twenty years will anyone still remember Gary Cooper when the tour leaders elaborate on the history of the area.

Towards the end of 1951 "Return to Paradise" was first considered. At that time Gary, fifty years of age, was not in the best of health. Separated from his wife Rocky, he had just received his second Academy Award for an outstanding performance in "High Noon".

The actor thought an extended visit to Europe might be the answer to his health problems and other worries. While on the Continent he sought a medical opinion and was told he had a duodenal ulcer.

Cooper returned to America in February, 1952, to visit his doctor in New Orleans before going into the Roosevelt Hospital in New York for treatment. Still with his ulcer but in better health the star then agreed to make the film in Samoa.

The first takes were made in mid-June, 1952, before the arrival of Cooper.

Earlier two American directors visited Western Samoa and picked Upolu as the location for the film. The producers said they would be looking for Samoan people to play certain parts in the film. They wanted to use as much local talent as possible because the story called for certain important scenes to be enacted

126

by Polynesian people. Lefaga with a beach front and village just off the shore made it the ideal location.

The movie concerns an American running away from society who stumbles on an island in the South Seas where he decides to live temporarily. Unattached, and wishing to be left alone, he finds on this island a degree of happiness that he has never known before.

The death of a woman of whom he has become fond causes the American to leave the island and wander around the Pacific for some fifteen years. The circumstances of World War II force him to return to his beloved island with a large store of provisions. When he ultimately realises that here is his true home he settles down there with the people and lives happily ever after.

More than 50 Americans arrived from overseas for the making of the film which was directed by Mark Robson, produced by Theron Warth, and released by United Artists.

Apart from Roberta Haynes, Gary Cooper, Barry Jones and Johnny Hudson, all the actors came from Samoa. Girls who were chosen for dance routines practised under Aggie Grey who also directed and taught Miss Haynes her dancing sequences.

"I practised with them nightly at the hotel," Aggie related. "The producers and directors were very pleased with our progress."

With the number of local castings for the motion picture, Apia was rapidly becoming film conscious. "Mt. Vaea may yet be renamed Beverly Hills of Samoa", was the joke of the time.

Accommodation of the company was divided between Aggie's and the Casino, managed by Mary.

At the airport the crowd gave Gary Cooper a tumultuous welcome when he arrived in Samoa on July 15 to make "Return to Paradise", which was his

82nd and first overseas film. There was such a melee at the airport that the actor was grateful for the shelter of his taxi when he set off for Apia. But Cooper and his friends were puzzled when the Samoan driver suddenly stopped the vehicle outside a *fale*. He beckoned a group of young children to the car. Addressing his distinguished passenger the driver said: "This is my family I want you to meet them."

"That was how Gary met his first Samoan family," Aggie chuckled. "He often spoke about the taxi driver's polite *aiga* and the unrehearsed Samoan welcome."

Filming started on July 25 and there were many other amusing happenings before the final takes.

There is a story of how the producer prepared a lot of small wooden wedges for jacking up dollies for camera equipment. Unable to find a place to store the wedges he stacked them near the dining room at the Casino. Searching next day he was staggered to learn that the wedges had been used for firewood by the kitchen staff.

One of the delights of the film set was the midday meal served by Aggie Grey and her staff. Every day in spite of transport and cooking difficulties the film crew were treated to excellent meals.

When the director of the film was leaving Samoa on October 9, 1952, he made a speech extolling the hospitality the company had received during their stay. He concluded by saying: "My earnest thanks go to Mrs. Aggie Grey for the manner in which she has looked after us all."

It was quite true what the director said. During their stay in Samoa, Gary Cooper and the film crew were truly overwhelmed by the friendship and kindness shown by Aggie. As a gesture of appreciation the film star presented Aggie with a *fale* which was built at the back of the hotel.

Several years later a very strong storm battered Apia Harbour, and wrecked the *fale*.

Anxious to improve conditions and make the hotel an important place in the life of Apia, Aggie decided that she should have a swimming pool. There had previously been a pool in Apia, in a private home, in fact the home in which Aggie herself had lived. Aggie decided the pool site should be on the exact position where the romantic Gary Cooper *fale* had been erected.

So construction commenced on what was to be known as Gary Cooper's swimming pool. Cement was an expensive item, but sand and water were plentiful. Foundation rods were also difficult to obtain, so the lack of rods and a cement mix which was weakened, brought about an unfortunate overnight transformation to the swimming pool.

After some weeks of construction work the swimming pool had been completed. It really did look something. It was raised off the ground with half-a-dozen steps leading up to the top of the pool wall, no arm supports. You just had to be good enough to find your way up those six steps and then drop into the pool.

It was opened with quite a flourish and christened by the TEAL airline crew who were staying overnight en route in the flying boat to Cook Islands and Tahiti. Everybody had a wonderful swim on the opening day. Aggie was toasted that night by everybody, even those who hadn't experienced the thrill of this new amenity.

Aggie herself had not yet taken the plunge. She got up early next morning, dressed in her *lavalava,* and made her way down to the pool. Climbing up the steps in readiness to dive into the water she was confronted by an empty pool with a gaping hole in the floor.

Lack of foundation rods plus the weight of the water and the frolicking on the opening day had caused the weak cement floor to subside during the night. All the water had seeped out and down through the volcanic ground — an absolute catastrophe.

Aggie was very disturbed at such a setback, but her son, Alan, quickly promised he would reconstruct the pool this time using foundation rods, which he did.

The pool stood for twenty-four years although it has not been used recently because guests would not wish to swim in a tank when a beautiful modern pool is only a few yards away.

Always it has been a good bet, though, that the old Gary Cooper swimming pool would stay forever on its sacred site at Aggie Grey's Hotel.

During August, 1978, to the amazement of old-timers the roar of pneumatic drills rattled the peaceful air not far from Aggie's bar. The swimming pool was being demolished. Aggie was standing by surveying the scene, her expression not showing her real feelings I'm sure.

"Aggie, I cannot believe my eyes, the pool is being cleared away," I gasped in amazement.

"Yes," replied Aggie in her deliberate way. "It is necessary now because the space is wanted for other things."

After the roar of the drills had paused for a while she added: "I'm not so worried because Alan has promised to build another small pool in a different position, so there will always be a Gary Cooper swimming pool.

"The making of 'Return to Paradise' was a most exciting time for us all. The crew were a happy carefree lot just like our own people. They were devoted to Gary Cooper, and I was too."

Aggie spoke of the letters she had exchanged with the film star after his return to America.

"He was very unhappy during the long separation from his wife and had often discussed these worries with me," she said. "I was so pleased to learn that after four years estrangement they had reunited in the summer of 1954.

"Gary Cooper was a fine ambassador of the United States and I'm sure he will always be remembered in Samoa. I felt very sad when I heard he had died on the 14th May, 1961."

Chapter 11

Mystery in the South Seas (1955-1961)

Like all great oceans of the world the Pacific has its share of unsolved secrets, none perhaps as mystifying as the story of the *Joyita*, a 75 ft. 70-ton twin-screw vessel.

Shortly after 5 a.m. on October 3, 1955, the commercial fisherboat chugged its way through the reef that protects Apia Harbour to begin the 280 mile journey to the New Zealand administered Tokelau Islands, a voyage of only three days.

There were twenty-five aboard the *Joyita*, nine listed as passengers and a crew of sixteen, none of whom seemed worried that one engine did not work and neither did the radio. She was skippered by a well-known South Seas identity, Captain "Dusty" Miller, in command for the last time, for the *Joyita* was fated never to reach her destination.

To this day a handful of locals who farewelled the ship from the Apia foreshore in a stormy October dawn were the last known to see the twenty-five people alive. The *Joyita* from that time onwards vanished for a period of thirty-six days.

In the sleepy Pacific world such deficiencies were fairly normal on vessels plying from one island paradise to another. Anyway, in this immense ocean the Tokelaus were really only just around the corner from Apia.

On the thirty-seventh morning she was found waterlogged and drifting about 450 miles west of Apia and more than 700 miles from her destination, the Tokelaus.

It was on November 10 that Captain Gerald Douglas, master of the Gilbertese island trader *Tuvalu*, sighted a derelict vessel and radioed his position to the Secretary of the Goverment in Tarawa. He reported that there was not a soul on board! The ship was the *Joyita* and it had foundered far off course — 160 miles north of the main Fiji group.

To this day the fate of the *Joyita's* company is a riddle. Not a single corpse was found, afloat or washed up.

Nor has there been any explanation why these people abandoned ship for the doubtful security of flimsy life rafts and why most of the cargo was missing.

Soon after discovery, the *Joyita* was towed to a nearby beach so that she could be pumped out. Refloated and carefully inspected, the ship assumed a still deeper mystery.

No holing of the hull was evident and there were certainly no bodies on board. The entire deck cargo was missing, so was an urgently needed consignment of aluminium stripping to be used on the trunks of coconut trees for rat prevention.

The stripping was in seven cases and had been stowed in the hold. Also gone from the hold were forty-four 150 lb. cases of flour, fifteen 70 lb. bags of sugar, eleven 56 lb. bags of rice and four hundred and sixty empty copra sacks.

Mr. G. K. Williams, listed on the manifest as a

supercargo, was carrying £1,000 for the purchase of Tokelau copra. Quite a sizeable sum of money in those days, it consisted of £50 in silver coins and £950 in bank notes. There was no trace of the £1,000.

Even more inexplicable was the fate of the 25 men on board. "Dusty" Miller had often boasted that with the cork in the holds the *Joyita* could not sink.

Yet it seemed she had been abandoned for the dubious safety of three flimsy rafts which were used by clinging to rope grips around the sides. Foul play seemed the only explanation.

On November 19, 1955, a Fiji newspaper carried a front page story alleging that "pirates" from a Russian submarine had looted the *Joyita* and killed passengers and crew.

Australian newpapers were more inclined to blame Japanese fishing boat crews. One sensational report had it that the men had "seen something the Japanese did not want them to see". As a result, bloodthirsty fishermen had stormed aboard and murdered everyone, then failed to sink the *Joyita*. The story was officially denied in Fiji, whose population disliked Japanese fishing crews. On the other hand Japanese newspapers did not bother to deny it, but commented acidly about "wild rumors" and "how silly people can be".

Other theorists came forward with arguments that a water spout had hit the *Joyita*, washing everyone overboard with such force that none could swim back. In support of this theory they pointed to the vessel's damaged superstructure. But experts who examined the damage believe it was caused by the ship wallowing for weeks in the pounding sea.

A similar theory was that the *Joyita* had been overwhelmed by a submarine earthquake. This was based on the fact that six months earlier another vessel, the *Hifafoa*, had been thrown on her beam ends by such an earthquake in the Tonga region. As the water erupted beneath her, 40-odd people on the *Hifafoa* were thrown overboard. All but one got back.

Prince Tungi of Tonga went on record with a belief that the *Joyita* had struck an uncharted reef, capsized and righted herself. "Those aboard," he said, "must have clung to her sides as long as they were able before the seas washed them away."

This theory did not explain the cargo missing from the holds or the disappearance of the compass, log book and charts. News that the compass, log and charts were missing led to a story that "Dusty" Miller had kidnapped his entire ship's company and whisked them away by raft to a desert island.

Even more far-fetched was a statement by an American, Dr. M. K. Jessup, that everyone could have been kidnapped by spacemen in flying saucers. Dr. Jessup was convinced that flying saucers had been careering round the skies for thousands of years, manned by usually harmless spacemen wanting to keep in touch with events on earth. He said that sometimes they captured humans to get a personal report from them, and preferred to take such hostages from ships or planes. This was the explanation of the *Mary Celeste* mystery, the doctor claimed.

The official enquiry into the *Joyita* mystery at Apia in February, 1956, cleared the air a little. Evidence was given that the flooding of the ship and the subsequent shutting off of the one serviceable engine had been caused by the corrosion and breaking of a one-inch galvanised pipe which formed part of the engine cooling system.

When the pipe sprang a leak, seawater was pumped by the engine into the holds at 2,000 gallons an hour.

By the time it was realised what was going on the water was so deep it was impossible to locate the leak and the only way to stop further flooding was to shut off the engine.

Although the enquiry gave one reason why the *Joyita* was found water-logged and adrift it could not determine what had then happened to the 25 passengers and crew.

The general assumption was that after drifting for some time "Dusty" Miller, possibly after the *Joyita* took a sudden list, panicked and gave the order to abandon ship. With him on a raft he took his compass, log and charts.

If that was the real explanation the missing men must have then perished in the shark-infested seas and the cargo looted later by islanders or some passing vessel.

On the beaches and in the bars of the South Pacific, however, there were many who would not accept these answers.

All who knew "Dusty" Miller in Apia swore he would never abandon his ship for the rafts. Indeed, it was because of his certainty that the *Joyita* was unsinkable that she carried no proper lifeboats.

Also there was no proper explanation why the *Joyita* had taken on more than 2,500 gallons of diesel fuel at Apia when she needed no more than 300 gallons for the run to the Tokelaus.

There's little similarity to the case of the *Marie Celeste* which was found in full sail in the Atlantic in 1872. Although not a soul was aboard that vessel, all else, however, was shipshape.

On the *Marie Celeste* there was an untouched meal laid ready on the crew's table. But practically everything had gone from the *Joyita* — the only food remaining was a slab of butter in a galley locker.

The *Joyita* had a glamorous beginning in 1931 when she was built by the Wilmington Boat Works in Los Angeles as an ocean-going yacht for Roland West, a Hollywood movie director. With an overall length of 75 feet and a beam of 17 feet, the vessel weighed 70 tons gross and 47 tons net. For a time she was owned by film star Mary Pickford.

Milton E. Bacon bought the *Joyita* in 1936. His widow who was interviewed when visiting Fiji gave a concise history of the ill-fated luxury yacht.

"*Joyita*" she said, "is a Mexican word meaning 'little jewel' and they pronounce it with an initial aspirate as '*Hoyita*'. She was one of the loveliest yachts you ever saw — the last word in luxury. Mr. West's wife's name was Jewel, and he really had the yacht built for her. Later he became involved with a famous film actress, Thelma Todd, who died mysteriously — another tragic chapter in the *Joyita* history.

"In 1936 my late husband, Mr. Bacon, bought the boat from Mr. West. What a wonderful time we had in her! All Thelma Todd's things were still in the yacht, and I often used them — her perfume bottles, toilet accessories, everything.

"Right up to 1941, we had great fun in the *Joyita* and then when we were sailing out of Santiago one day, the Navy came along, requisitioned her and took her to Pearl Harbor, where she was on patrol during the war. No expense was spared in building or equipping her. In the old days she had the latest navigation aids, including an automatic pilot, twin diesel engines, a huge deep-freeze, great ice boxes, and tanks for 2,500 gallons of water and 3,000 gallons of fuel. She was a superb sea-boat for cruising or fishing, and was equipped with fishing chairs."

On U.S. Navy patrol in 1943 the *Joyita* suffered a

grounding that necessitated replanking much of the lower part of the hull. After she was declared surplus to Navy needs in 1946, the *Joyita* was sold to buyers who converted the vessel for commercial fishing. Refrigeration was installed and two 225 h.p. diesel engines fitted.

In 1952 the *Joyita* was sold to Dr. Ellen Luomala of Honolulu. Several weeks later "Dusty" Miller chartered the ship with a view to operating it in the South Seas.

Dr. Luomala and "Dusty" Miller became friendly. He referred to her as his fiancee; it was understood they would marry when his Welsh wife divorced him.

One of Miller's money-making schemes was to use the *Joyita* for commercial fishing. For this purpose he had her holds insulated with five-inch cork for storage of frozen fish.

The fishing venture did not pay off. By mid 1955, after some charter work around the islands, Miller was stranded in Apia and future prospects looked gloomy.

In September, 1955, "Dusty" was in really dire straits. He was heavily in debt and could not sail into the port of Pago Pago where there were writs waiting his appearance. When an Apia firm urgently needed a charter vessel for the Tokelau run "Dusty" saw this as a last opportunity to clear his name. At all costs it seemed, he was prepared to make this voyage.

Aggie told me that "Dusty" had done some odd jobs around the hotel and was often in the bar.

"Miller was about 39 years of age", she recalled. "He came from a long line of sea-faring people and served with the British Merchant Marine for the greater part of his life. He said he enlisted at the age of 14 and at the outbreak of war transferred to the

Royal Navy Volunteer Reserve, serving in various capacities, and finally being demobolised with the rank of lieutenant-commander. Following his discharge he sailed around the Pacific and then finally took a charter of the *Joyita* for fishing operations. And it was here in Apia that I first met Miller."

Kurt Stunzner talked to me about how he should have been aboard the *Joyita* on its ill-fated voyage. A well-known old-timer and a very good friend of mine, Kurt was employed by the Government in the Health Department. From time to time many difficult jobs seemed to come his way.

Just prior to the departure of the *Joyita* a signal had been received from the Tokelaus that there was a plague of rats in the islands. Kurt was to go and supervise the eradication.

A few hours before sailing time his trip was cancelled when a sudden outbreak of influenza required his presence at the Apia hospital.

Both Kurt and Aggie had an idea that someone in Apia was doing some maintenance work on a pump on the *Joyita* and if "Dusty" had been sufficiently patient to wait for the repair to be completed then many say she may not have sunk.

I asked Fred Fairman about this story. "I don't know about the job on the pump but 'Dusty' left Apia in a mighty hurry," he said, "I knew him quite well as he had been waiting around for a long time hoping against hope for a charter. The Tokelau opportunity was offered him just when he was at desperation point. I'm inclined to think that some person on board may have gone mad and killed everyone else and done away with himself."

In 1956 the *Joyita* was bought for £2425 by a Fiji planter who spent another £6,000 fitting her as an island trading vessel.

Within six months she piled up on Horseshoe Reef, in the Koro Sea. She was refloated and repaired but in 1959 grounded again on the reef at Vatuvula, Fiji.

She was towed to Levuka. Her engines and fittings were removed and she was abandoned.

In November, 1960, came an epilogue when, in a court in Cardiff, Wales, "Dusty" Miller's wife sought a divorce on grounds of desertion or presumption of death.

The judge said: "The respondent and his crew have gone to the bottom of the sea. There is evidence of the presumption that he is dead and on those grounds I grant Mrs. Miller a decree nisi."

*   *   *

About 1955 with the completion of her first real expansion — the construction of the little units adjacent the main building — Aggie began to think of more ways to bring tourists to Apia.

TEAL, later to be re-named Air New Zealand, were flying the original Coral Route from Auckland to Suva, Western Samoa, Cook Islands and Tahiti. The wonderful Solent flying-boats, brought absolute luxury travel. To visit the islands this way was something to remember. Each trip brought a few tourists, and with the crew, they stayed at Aggie's overnight.

Aggie remembered that one of her early flights happened by accident. She was in Suva and unfortunately missed the *Tofua* on its way to Apia, so decided to travel on the TEAL flying-boat. She recalled how they were only a short way out of Suva when the stewardess said unfortunately the plane had to return to Fiji because of bad weather in Western Samoa.

Aggie had been speaking on the telephone to Apia earlier that morning and understood the weather was perfect, so she expressed some amazement at this decision. It was not until they landed in the water of Suva Harbour at Laucala Bay that the passengers were aware one motor was not operating. As a considerable amount of maintenance was necessary, their flight was cancelled until the next morning.

However, all had an enjoyable time billeted at the legendary GPH hotel. Next day one of those smooth uneventful flights for which the flying-boats were renowned, brought Aggie home to Western Samoa.

The Solents landed at Satapuala about 20 miles from Apia and a short distance from the present airport at Faleolo. For the transit passengers there were few formalities. Spending an overnight stop at Aggies was one of the bonus highlights of the TEAL Coral route.

Immigration rules insisted that disembarking passengers staying in Samoa must leave any alcoholic liquor for lodgement in the local bond store.

Even opened bottles received this treatment and the government officers marked the tide level in the bottle with a pencil. Departing travellers insisted that although the level of their liquor usually looked the same when they sampled it back on board the aircraft there was invariably a distinct loss of strength in the tasting.

Aggie's Hotel didn't have the modern conveniences of today; in fact the top floor was often likened to a stable with perhaps less divisions. For sure, the sleeping area had about as much privacy as a Samoan toilet block.

The broadminded air crews of those days were

tolerant, realising that the hospitality at Aggies compensated for most of these short-comings.

In 1955 there were four hotels in Apia, all un-licensed. There was the Casino, operated by the New Zealand Reparation Estates, boasting rooms with hand-basins and two showers and toilet facilities. The tariff, including meals, was twenty-eight shillings per day (US$4 at that time).

There was the White Horse Inn, about a mile from the General Post Office. Located away from the seafront, the Inn didn't have any rooms with running water but there was a tennis court in reasonable condition.

The Heather Bell Hotel was located on the bay near where the deep-sea wharf now stands. Nearby was the Matautu Village renowned in modern times for its dancing girls.

Of course Aggie Grey's Hotel was the popular place to stay. It was the automatic selection for air crews, transit passengers and tourists.

Liquor was really scarce, supposedly for medicinal purposes. The police commissioner had considerable latitude in handing out the necessary points to purchase supplies.

Visitors were fairly treated except that transit passengers were unable to obtain permits. Although the European residents received their points there were however few Samoans sufficiently fortunate to be considered up to the necessary 'standard'.

It is difficult to imagine the conditions of a quarter of a century ago. Many tourists nowadays would catch the next plane out of a country where authorities took away their favourite bottles at the airport. Especially angry were the visitors who anxiously awaited the handing back of their temporarily confiscated bottle only to be told "We are sorry, sir, but your liquor has been left in town (20 miles away) at the bond store. It is not possible to get it now because of the distance and there is no telephone from here to the store."

Aggie Grey, like the other hotelkeepers, could not obtain liquor points for their guests. So that she could build up a small bar stock Aggie urged all visitors to claim their points. Kindly non-drinkers helped supplies considerably and usually all arriving guests at the hotel could get a cold beer. It was an unwritten law that when you checked out you gave Aggie the unused balance of your valuable rations.

In 1955 the tariff at Aggie's Hotel was also twenty-eight shillings a day per person for a double room. Singles were thirty-two shillings and six pence. Apart from the rooms there were two cottages. Only these two had private bathrooms.

For US$4 a day you had a bed, morning and afternoon tea, breakfast, lunch and dinner. Who wanted a private bathroom?

Occasionally airline passengers raised mildly-voiced objections to undressing in their cubicles behind partitions barely five feet high. Generally times and people could be organised so as to suit, but it seems that some of the ladies objected to having to undress in a more-or-less crouched position so that only their head showed above the bedroom's semi-wall.

Before very long Aggie was convinced that Samoan *fale* conditions didn't necessarily apply to Samoan hotels. Something would have to be done quickly, before even the outstanding Aggie Grey hospitality proved an insufficient incentive to counteract the complaints of a minority of the tourists.

Money was again in short supply — as it remained for a long time, but Aggie has plenty of friends. It

143

wasn't long before an ingenious scheme guaranteed that the top floor and other parts of the hotel could be brought a little closer to two-star standards.

Timber was the main ingredient needed, but good quality oregon was scarce and expensive, far beyond the Grey purse. Aggie had made a lot of money with the wartime hamburgers, but this was used to establish the hotel and consolidate her investments. There was a limit to how much could now be spent.

For ages Thor ships have been calling at Apia in their voyages from America's west coast through the islands of the South Pacific. Only in the mid-seventies did the last of the line berth in Western Samoa.

The officers and crew were unanimous in their acclaim of the nights of hospitality at Aggies. Always there was a *fiafia* when the ships were in port, always an outstanding night for the small cluster of round-trip passengers lucky enough to have obtained passages on a Thor ship.

Aggie related how it was agreed that whenever a Thor ship anchored in Apia Harbour it would be found urgently necessary for the crew to unload some of their surplus dunnage.

Selected pieces of choice timber were lashed together and lowered over the side of the ship. Times were chosen during the days and often at night when tides were right to float the rafts to the shore.

"It didn't take much practice to work out the currents so that the rafts landed as close as possible to our front door," said Aggie.

"Each ship brought us a nice load of beautiful timber and we completed a number of projects to improve the hotel and make things more comfortable for the guests.

"Just when we were putting the finishing touches to the top floor bedrooms the police learned about our Apia Harbour rafts and caught us red-handed. The judge agreed with the police that this timber was indeed a prohibited importation because we had no licence. Despite my protestations that it was unwanted dunnage which by Providence had found its way to our front door, I was fined five pounds," said Aggie ruefully, but with that twinkle in her eye.

This was about the time that Sir Gordon Taylor was trying to establish a regular flying boat charter service through the South Pacific as far as Tahiti. Sir Gordon is well known for his pioneer flights across the Pacific between the US and Australia on his own and in association with Sir Charles Kingsford Smith.

He was awarded the George Cross, a high British Empire award for exceptional bravery when flying with Kingsford Smith from Sydney to New Zealand in 1935. They were carrying a large Jubilee air mail, much of which was jettisoned when the *Southern Cross* suffered the loss of a motor 600 miles from Sydney.

Taylor transferred oil from the defective motor in mid-air, edging his way across the aircraft wing. His epic action saved the *Southern Cross*.

Sir Gordon told me in his Sydney office that everything he wrote about Aggie in his book "Bird of the Islands" was true. "These are my heartfelt sentiments of the wonderful times we had in Apia," he said "It was where we spent the happiest days in the Pacific".

In his book about *Frigate Bird III* Sir Gordon wrote: "We more or less took over Aggie Grey's Hotel. This is a place of great personality surpassed in Samoa only by its proprietress, Mrs. Aggie Grey.

"A clean white-painted timber house on the sea front at Apia, it is the genuine South Sea Island Hotel; cool and airy, open passages and doorways hung with bamboo blinds and with silent pandanus mats upon the floors; air-conditioned by the trade winds from the ocean and by the shade of trees which spread high over its lawns. Aggie Grey's and Samoa were another experience . . ."

Aggie had fond memories of Sir Gordon's visits to her hotel, as they were always such a happy group. "Taylor liked quietude," recalled Aggie, "and he would often leave gatherings that were inclined to be noisy to drive off to a place of solitude".

Aggie thought he was too late with his attempts to create a flying-boat service. "The operational costs were soaring and we were all so very sorry when his Catalina flights were discontinued," she said.

Harry Purvis was co-pilot to Sir Gordon Taylor in many of his Pacific flights. He began flying in 1929, pioneering many air routes, particularly in the outback. He was with Taylor on the first aircraft to fly from Australia to South America and return in 1951.

I asked Harry about his times with Aggie Grey — did he remember much, was he impressed? In a flash he exclaimed "Who, passing through Apia, did not carry away memories of this fabulous woman?

"We stayed overnight always with her, some forty people on our way to Tahiti and it never failed to be an experience. She had the hotel and the trading store next door and we always saw to it that our passengers had time to make purchases from her amazing collections of handicrafts from as far away as the Tokelaus".

Purvis vividly remembered the hotel as a regular gathering place for Aggie's many friends who seemed to appear from everywhere at dusk. "They seemed unlimited. They were happy and carefree — Aggie's hospitality must have been infectious, effecting her friends the same way as it did us."

I asked Harry about the renowned service at Aggie's and he told me that nothing was too much trouble in that atmosphere of the true South Seas. Food was excellent, and always there was a *fiafia* and other entertainment with a duration limited only by a dawn departure.

With a smile on his suntanned face (he was in Alice Springs — the centre of Australia) Harry recalled Aggie's comments after she returned to Apia following a serious internal operation. "I asked her how she felt after this serious surgery," explained Purvis. Aggie answered with a chuckle, "Harry, after the op, I feel like a new man!"

The last Solent flying-boat of Air New Zealand went to its final home in Auckland in May 1966. The "boat" which flew three million miles and 14,500 hours on the South Pacific passenger services from 1949-1960 has been restored as an exhibit of the Auckland Museum of Transport and Technology. It had been "on the hard" at Hobsonville RNZAF station since being withdrawn in 1960 from the Suva-Tahiti service.

Air New Zealand flew five Short Solents before converting to DC6s in 1954 but they retained one Solent to operate their "Coral Route" to Tahiti via Western Samoa and the Cook Islands until September 1960. Of the other four aircraft two were sold to Aquila Airways in the UK and two were scrapped.

The 80 miles between Apia and Pago were still serviced as they had been for ages by island boats with absolutely no comfort of any sort. True enough the passage was low-priced to suit the pocket of the Samoans, but hardly up to standards expected on even the lowest tourist budget.

Since the end of World War II there were airstrips at Pago and Faleolo, site of the present airport, but no service operated between the two points. Obviously here was a link that had to be forged even if it meant that Aggie had to back a promoter willing to fly the route.

One can be excused from thinking it would be a simple matter to establish an 80-mile air route even in the still remote South Pacific islands, especially when the two serviceable airstrips were ready, an aeroplane available, and there existed an acute need for a scheduled service between the two points.

The inauguration of the Pago-Apia air link involved businessmen, government officials, backers, airlines with aircraft, wishful-thinkers with get-rich-quick ideas, the New Zealand Department of Civil Aviation (on the Western Samoa side) and the FAA (for American Samoa), plus many interested sideline parties.

Probably no air service in the Pacific had a more difficult and frustrating birth. Individuals and companies went bankrupt while negotiations dragged on for months and months without the bureaucracy reaching an agreement.

The early establishment of the service was of great concern to the traders in Apia, particularly those interested in tourist promotion like the Gold Star Company and Aggie Grey.

"It was essential that we had some means of transport that was comfortable, quick and reliable, so that tourists could conveniently come from Pago to Apia", explained Aggie. "You could not expect American tourists to roll on the deck like sacks of copra. Sometimes in bad weather the *Sulimoni* and the *Annabelle Rose* took eight or ten hours. When they reached Apia at 3 a.m. it needed a mighty good *fa'a-Samoa* welcome to convince them they had done the right thing to come to Western Samoa.

"When I think about it I guess we didn't really have many disgruntled visitors. After a day they usually boasted of the way they had to rough it to reach an off-the-beaten-track place like Apia.

"For me the most important aspect was the fact that there were dozens of potential tourists arriving regularly in Pago by Pan American Airways. They were using DC4 and Strato-cruisers and were publicising American Samoa as a new holiday paradise. Of course there was no mention of Western Samoa.

"Mainly it was a transport problem, although there were often frustrating difficulties in tourists getting an entry visa at short notice. But that's a different story," shrugged Aggie.

An unknown hero, certainly unsung and perhaps unrewarded, in the saga of the establishment of Polynesian Air Lines was Australian airman Reginald Barnewall.

In 1958, Reg came to Apia chockful of ambitions to establish with a minimum of delay an air service across those 80 miles of sea.

A syndicate of local investors was planning to use a Grumman Mallard. There were the inevitable delays at Government levels, generally wrangles associated with reciprocal rights.

New Zealand, the administrators of civil aviation in Western Samoa, and the American authorities both knew that there was not room for two airlines operating the short haul. One might survive, but if there were two, then both would ultimately fail.

Both of the negotiating bodies also knew that the first airline to begin operations held a decided advantage.

The Americans submitted their blueprint for a US company, Samoan Airlines, to inaugurate the service with a 31-passenger DC3 chartered from Hawaiian

Airlines. In fact the service did begin. Then the New Zealand authorities withheld their approval for a licence renewal for so long that the American operators went bankrupt.

Wishful-thinking is a popular ingredient of life in the South Seas. It can be bracketed with another favourite solution to Polynesian problems — munyana.

It didn't take Barnewall long to realise that above all patience is essentially the lifesaver in Pacific island arbitration.

Barnewall was patient. After he saw the Grumman proposal disintegrate, he was most disappointed when the Americans with their DC3 announced they were ready to operate. Then came a respite when a landing authority for the Pago-based company did not arrive.

With independence less than three years away, it seems certain now that the Western Samoa Government exercised its influence with New Zealand to delay the DCA permission as long as possible.

Behind the scenes the same syndicate of Apia traders was quietly working towards buying an aircraft that would suit their needs. Barnewall with his patience was well in the picture.

"He stayed at my hotel for quite a time, until he was allocated a government house," Aggie recounted. "I had many meetings with Reg and although I sympathised with his troubles, my main concern was for someone to inaugurate the air service, especially as TEAL had announced they would soon withdraw their Solent flying-boat."

At the beginning of March, 1959, Barnewall had been trying to buy a de Havilland *Dove* aircraft from the defunct Southern Air Lines in Australia.

He wrote to his oldtime buddy Bernie ("Beeswax") Beswicke offering him the job of chief engineer of

Polynesian Airlines — if it finally became airborne. Reg was most anxious for "Beeswax" to accept because he knew his capabilities. Furthermore to have someone in Australia chasing spare parts, tools, and other necessary gear was the ideal situation.

By the beginning of May the syndicate were still undecided on the purchase of the aircraft. In addition to the Southern Air Lines *Dove*, there was a Percival *Prince* available from an Australian aero club.

At a meeting of the investors on May 7, 1959, important conclusions resulted in a vote in favour of the *Prince*.

Barnewall cabled the news to his friend "Beeswax" on May 16 and followed with a lengthy letter next day. So Polynesian Airlines was in business — a shoestring airline, destined to remain in that sad state for many years to come.

"When I heard the report of the meeting and the purchase of the plane," Aggie recalled, "I didn't get over-excited. There had been so many rumours and false starts that I pledged there would be no celebrations until the service really commenced."

Samoan Airlines, the American company, began flying their DC3 Viewmaster between Pago and Apia late in 1959. They had twice-daily flights except on Thursdays with a fare of £7 return. In Apia well-known identity Peter Plowman was their agent.

Polynesian Airlines had applied for operating rights and received permission from New Zealand in September, 1959. No approval had been received from the American side and the matter was subject to protracted negotiations between NZ and the US.

At the time it did seem that the Pago-based airline had stolen a march on the Western Samoans. Then in February, 1960, their DC3 was damaged and the service stopped.

Although Polynesian Airlines did not have authorisation to land at Pago they began their service with the Percival *Prince*. It was reported: "Polynesian Airlines thought that their permission had been granted so they commenced flying passengers to meet connecting air services."

Very soon the American Samoa Government put a stop to Polynesian Airlines — no landing permission yet granted.

"These moves were all political," said Aggie. "All we wanted were regular flights connecting with Pago, not stop-and-go schedules as were happening. All sorts of rumours were heard. A most amusing story was that Governor Peter Coleman of American Samoa was a brother of Lawrence Coleman, director of Samoan Airlines. This was very quickly officially denied in Pago."

In March, 1960, Polynesian Airlines officially commenced their regular service between the two Samoas. They scheduled a return flight every day except Sunday.

When Samoan Airlines were ready to operate again following the damage to their DC3 it was their turn to face a rude shock. Western Samoan authorities advised them that landing in Apia was refused because they did not have a "1960-dated permit" from NZ.

Somehow or other the new authorisation never did arrive. Permission was never refused, only deferred. The application seemed glued to the pigeon hole where it was carefully filed. Because of the delay Samoan Airlines eventually went bankrupt and their aircraft was returned to Hawaii. Then Polynesian Airlines had the route to themselves and kept it that way for many years to come.

*   *   *

Warnings were sent to the islands of the South Seas to expect tidal waves at a certain date. In Samoa everyone believed such forecasts were often guesswork. But on May 22, 1960, it happened . . .

Aggie described how she was watching out to sea from the hotel.

"I noticed a mighty swell on the distant horizon," she said. "As I stared the great mountain of water came closer and closer.

"I called a warning and by this time many other people were gazing out to sea. Most watchers then realised this was the tidal wave."

The mighty rollers struck the Apia foreshore with the greatest velocity at the mouth of the Vaisigano River that flows alongside of Aggie's Hotel.

"In a matter of seconds," continued Aggie, "the level of the river rose a dozen feet as the water tore straight up the mouth, carrying everything in front of it."

All sorts of fish jostled with Samoan *paopao* and other fishing craft as they all rode at breakneck speed on to the beach. When the water receded it left along the reef thousands of colourful fish of countless types. There were eels and sharks of all sizes tossed around in the whirling currents unable to withstand the tremendous forces built up by the tides over thousands of miles of ocean. The tidal wave followed an eruption in Chile.

Altogether there had been about nine really tremendous waves before the water receded so much that it left Apia Harbour almost dry. Along the foreshore people were running into the harbour basin and out to the reef.

"No-one seemed to realise the water might come back at any time and many would drown," said Aggie. "I was just as foolish, because I was one of the first to reach the reef. After a short time fossicking among the coral I decided I best get back to the foreshore as soon as possible."

Luckily the water did not return with a rush so the harbour was refilled slowly. In a space of about thirty minutes everything looked normal again.

There was not much local damage — nothing like a hurricane — although conditions had been hectic and worrying in the short period. Many outlying villages at the water's edge suffered considerable damage but there was no loss of life.

*   *   *

Aggie had made many improvements to her property by 1960. Shrubs and glorious tropical trees had been planted and it seemed it was time for more units to be erected to cater for the gradual build up of tourists.

"We hadn't much increased our available accommodation since the cottages built near Gary Cooper's pool in 1954," Aggie explained. "So I thought it was about time we made another move. We built a row of single-storey units beginning underneath the hotel kitchen and extending down past Alan's house to the back of our property."

These units were really the beginning of the tremendous expansion in Aggie's hotel property. Every year or so saw another block of units opened to tourists. But in 1960 not even Aggie could have visualised her incredible tropical complex as it would exist at the end of the seventies.

*   *   *

Meanwhile, over the years, Samoa's rocky road to independence was gradually being smoothed.

154

The United Nations in 1960 were becoming more active in the plans to give the little country complete freedom. After all, said some commentators, the *Mau* Movement had its beginning in real earnest in 1926 when the legendary OF organised publication of the *Samoa Guardian* printed in the purple colours of the movement — the first newspaper in the Samoan language.

In 1960, the Prime Minister, Fiame Mata'afa Faumuina, addressed the Trusteeship Council at UN. In an impassioned plea for Western Samoa, Mata'afa said his people had never since the days of the German occupation ever wavered from their aim to be a free and independent nation.

In fact, he said, in the earlier days even under New Zealand rule there had been armed conflicts because of this fierce desire for independence. But, Mata'afa continued, times had changed so much that Samoa, New Zealand and the UN had, since 1946, been working harmoniously towards complete freedom for his people. Now the time had come.

The New Zealand Government agreed with the Samoan Prime Minister so it was up to UN to give a ruling.

The UN generally approved any applications for independence when it came from a universally elected government. When this was not the case, as with Samoa, UN required a plebiscite at which every person of age was given the right to vote.

Before independence the Samoans had no nationality of their own but were protected persons of New Zealand. Non-Samoans and ex-patriots practically all had their own nationalities.

There was to be no provision after independence for dual citizenships. Residents had to decide whether to apply for Samoan citizenship and this depended on their birthplace, descendants, naturalisation or registration.

Dr. Najmuddine Rifai, a doctor of philosophy in international law, from the United Arab Republic, was the UN plebiscite commissioner. With his team of 12 UN staff members they were in Samoa for four weeks touring the country so as to register the people to vote and make sure they understood the terms of the plebiscite.

Everything was being done to acquaint the Samoans with the particulars of the new constitution. Radio time was provided for the "yes" and "no" advocates; there were many public meetings continuing late into the night.

In a radio speech, Tupua Tamasese Mea'ole, who became joint Head of State, spoke in favour of independence saying, "A plebiscite is a change to our established custom and foreign to Samoans. Is this not what is called outside interference? Vote 'yes' so that never again will there be interference with us from abroad."

The plebiscite was held on May 9, 1961, and resulted in an overwhelming decision in favour of independence. Nearly 90% of the registered people exercised their right to vote.

Western Samoa was to become an independent state on January 1, 1962.

Chapter 12

Independence (1962-1967)

New Year's Eve, 1961, was celebrated with even greater revelry than is usual in Apia for it heralded the first day of independence for the little nation.

For those oldtime leaders of the now defunct *Mau* it was a wonderful time, an achievement that in the thirties many thought an impossibility. But they never gave up nor wavered in their ambition to achieve their freedom goal.

To a select few it was a triumph for they had worked untiringly, always hoping that the rest of the world would, through the UN, give Samoa a chance to completely control their own affairs. Unlike 1920 and 1946, this time the Samoan people were having a say in their future.

The strain of making visits to the UN in New York must have seemed all worthwhile to the joint Heads of State — Tupua Tamasese Mea'ole and Malietoa Tanumafile II. Not that making speeches was any great problem to these important dignitaries, but it must be remembered they were in strange and unknown surroundings, amongst representatives of powers then not entirely in favour of the complete independence movement being pleaded at UN.

For the four daughters of O. F. Nelson January 1, 1962, must have been a wonderful day. The support and faith they had demonstrated for their father had been worthwhile — now Samoa was truly and entirely a free land. For Fiame Mata'afa Faumuina, the Prime Minister who was a strictly religious person, his faith in God had been rewarded. Mata'afa, whose father had been President of the *Mau*, proved the ideal leader at this time for the new nation.

"His father, Faumuina Mulinu'u I, maintained a strict discipline in the village of Lepea," Aggie told me. "It was a control typical of the older days. For instance, no-one in the village would dare light up his *fale* until a light had appeared in the house of Faumuina.

"Then at bedtime, as soon as his lights were extinguished, all other lights in the village would be put out immediately." Aggie thought conditions had changed after the death of Faumuina.

"Under Mata'afa's rule the discipline was relaxed somewhat but he too was always accorded the greatest respect due to a paramount chief," was her opinion.

Another whose thoughts on Independence Day would have been a kaleidoscope of the sad and gallant deeds of the past was Fa'alava'au Galu. Fa'alava'au, who had been the secretary of the *Mau*, was the first Minister of Posts. He held this portfolio for a number of years and I often talked with him. A kindly, softly spoken gentleman, you didn't have to be told he was a high chief. You knew immediately you saw him.

When the 1962 independence celebrations had drawn to a close many New Zealand Government workers left Samoa. The new Administration had to face up to many problems.

Prime Minister Mata'afa gave his people some good advice when he said, "We cannot effectively bring peace to other independent states by providing economic assistance, or by supplying them with weapons of warfare, but we can show a shining example of a people living in peace and harmony, something rarely found in other countries today.

"We must maintain our ways and traditions because they teach every Samoan the virtue of courtesy, and promote a respectful attitude towards one's fellow men."

Aggie thought these words of Mata'afa to be very true. "After independence I felt we would have many tourists visiting Apia, so I planned more extensions and hoped we could fill the rooms with new visitors."

They decided to build another line of single storey units along the Vaisigano River boundary of the property. "This left ample space in the centre because I hoped one day we might have a large guest *fale* of genuine Samoan construction," said Aggie.

In 1962 this next line of units was opened. It increased Aggie's accommodation to 60 beds. Aggie's was the place to stay in Samoa — now there was no real competition. The Casino was not favoured by tourists. Mostly it was occupied by long-term expatriates at special monthly tariffs.

Aggie then had, and continues to have, a very firm policy that the girls of the villages and ones of doubtful morals in town must not enter the hotel compound area during the daytime and of course most definitely not at night.

Many amusing incidents must have occurred over the years but one during the sixties concerned quite a high American official from the hospital at Pago Pago and his buddy.

Not only did the night watchman maintain a very tight security on the admission of the village girls after hours, but most of Aggie's employees were alerted in case any unsavoury characters were brought into the hotel by gleeful guests anticipating an entertaining evening in their rooms.

A Solomon Island girl on Aggie's staff with a disturbingly powerful physique was a particularly faithful backer of the hotel policy. She was on duty one evening when the two Americans arrived at the hotel with three girls who were quickly judged to be on the doubtful list. After due warning from Aggie's girls the ladies of the town refused to leave, so Aggie's girls set about evicting them in a persuasive Samoan style which immediately developed into a fight.

The two Americans, naturally rather disturbed at the possible loss of the happy times anticipated by them for later that evening, joined the fight. The encounter was rather short, and the village girls quickly left. But during the disturbance one of the Americans was thrown in the swimming pool, receiving not only a ducking, but was hauled out of the water with a broken leg.

As he was attached to the hospital in Pago Pago there was no difficulty in obtaining treatment when he returned, but it would be interesting to know exactly what excuse he gave for having arrived in Pago in that condition after being away for "a couple of days healthy relaxation" in Western Samoa.

Aggie was busy planning more extensions to the hotel. It seemed there was no limit to the number of guests who could be accommodated provided the money could be found for the new buildings.

This was a problem because although success was snowballing the money was needed to repay the cost of earlier improvements. Somehow the inimitable Aggie arranged finance and the foundations were laid for another block of units.

When the new wing of two storeys was opened

towards the end of 1965 it gave Aggie a total of 45 rooms capable of accommodating 76 people.

This latest addition costing £12,000 immediately became the most popular area for guests who revelled in the luxury of the eight twin-bedded rooms. Each room had every known Pacific hotel convenience — airconditioning, electric fan, refrigerator, shower and toilet facilities and a telephone.

The absence of piped music was appreciated by the guests who found it more pleasant to sit quietly at the bar tables while Aggie's musicians entertained with romantic South Sea island songs.

*   *   *

The Constitution of Western Samoa provided that should a joint Head of State die then the surviving head would rule the nation. On April 15, 1963, Tupua Tamasese Mea'ole died from lung cancer. Malietoa Tanumafili II then became the sole Head of State. On his death Tamasese's place in the four man Council of Deputies made up of the four highest chiefs of Samoa became vacant.

Two claimants appeared for the vacant title and a dispute arose as to whether the Tupua title, the Tamasese title, or the joint Tupua Tamasese title was the royal one.

The first public announcement on the title came from the Minister of Justice, Tuatagaloa Leutele Te'o. As spokesman of the Safenuinuivao family of Falefa and Salani, he claimed their hereditary right to bestow the Tupua title. He made known that the family's choice was Dr. Lealofi Tamasese, a nephew of Mea'ole and the son of Tupua Tamasese Lealofi, who was shot and killed by New Zealand police in Beach Road during the *Mau* disturbances in 1929.

Very soon there was a counter-claim from the Sa Tuala and other related families to support Tufuga Efi Tamasese, son of Mea'ole, for the royal title.

For the overseas visitor the intense interest paid by Samoans to the hearings of the Lands and Titles Court is often difficult to understand. Yet it is in this court that decisions are made affecting so many important facets of life in the nation.

Apart from deciding disputes on titlement to land, the judges also bring down decisions on the rights of persons to hold titles. In recent years perhaps one of the most important was the Court's selection of the man who would then become one of four eligible to be Head of State on the death of the present ruler, Malietoa Tanumafili II — in effect the next king of Samoa.

To the average Samoan having no family connections with either claimant, Efi and Lealofi both appeared to have the required qualifications to become a member of the Council of Deputies. As can be imagined in cases such as this, each family gives unrelenting support to their respective candidates. Any of the *aiga* would be thought a traitor if he failed in this regard.

Giving a reserved decision after four days of hearings, the court found that the title Tupua, formerly held by the late Head of State, Tupua Tamasese Mea'ole, is a royal title of the *Tama-a-aiga*; the right to confer this title lay with the Sa Fenuinuivao family: and Lealofi Tupua Tamasese was therefore rightful holder of the title.

*   *   *

One of the greatest adventurers of modern times to visit Western Samoa was the 71-year-old William

Willis who sailed his raft *Age Unlimited* from Peru to Australia.

Willis started his life in Germany and first went to sea in the square-riggers of 1908 when he was 15. His fearless love of the sea and its complexities enabled him to master challenges that verged on the impossible.

In his raft *Age Unlimited* Willis left Callao, Peru, on July 4, 1963, bound for Australia. He completed the long first stage on November 12, 1963, when his raft, flying a distress signal, landed near Apia. The 1-ton steel vessel required repairs resulting from storm damage and Willis himself was in urgent need of medical attention. The lay-over in Samoa was a long one and it was not until June 29, 1964, that the lone sailor left Apia.

When he was in Apia he made many friends among the Samoan people.

"I knew him well," recalled Aggie. "I was one of the first people to greet Willis when he arrived in Apia. I thought he was a wonderful old gentleman and so very courageous. He was very popular with the Samoan people. Being sailors in the early days they admired Willis because he had sailed the raft single-handed all the way from South America."

Willis stayed at Aggie's and they spent a long time together talking about his experiences. "I felt very sad when I learned that he was lost at sea somewhere in the Atlantic Ocean," Aggie added.

The alert Western Samoa Post Office was aware of the possible philatelic interest to be created by a Samoa-Australia raft mail. A closing time was advertised for an official mail and a bag of 421 articles cancelled June 20, 1964, was handed over to Willis.

He arrived on the Australian continent when he beached the *Age Unlimited* at Tully in Northern

Queensland on September 9. During the 2½ months he had been at sea after leaving Samoa there had been only one report of a ship sighting the raft. This came on August 18 from the freighter *Baron Jedburgh* near, strangely enough, Willis Island some 250 miles east of Cairns.

When he grounded his raft on that lonely stretch of beach, the *Age Unlimited* was flying the distress signal and the mainsail was in tatters.

Willis was concerned there wasn't a welcoming party, in fact there was nobody there to greet him. It was almost five hours before somebody wandered along the beach and saw the intrepid explorer. During the morning, before he arrived, Willis had fired distress rockets but none were seen from the Tully township.

Tully schoolmaster, Hank Penning and his wife, who lived at the mouth of the Tully River, were the first Australians to meet him. They saw a stranger across the mouth of the Tully River and waved. Penning crossed the river in his boat. Willis introduced himself saying, "I'm Willis from New York."

*   *   *

In the period from independence until 1964 Samoa had been inundated with experts from UN, WHO, FAO, and other similar associated well meaning bodies. The highly dollar-paid specialists came and went — produced volumes of reports which probably are still gathering dust on their white and coloured ribboned manila folders. At one stage there were about 20 UN experts working in various fields.

When the experts left Samoa many felt their mission had been unsatisfactory. If they did not achieve the results that were expected of them, then the usual excuse was to blame the Samoan people or the *matai* system.

When he left after a two-year FAO term, agriculture adviser F. C. Panganiban announced that the *matai* system made agricultural development in Western Samoa well nigh impossible.

So many experts blamed the Samoan people or the social and economic inequalities when they should have sought other solutions to the problems. Some specialists thought up fantastic ideas. A UN adviser in 1964 announced that Samoan tobacco lent itself well to the making of cigars. According to expert J. J. van der Goes a Samoan agriculture department official might be sent to the Philippines for training in cottage style cigar making.

Van der Goes advised the Government that with very little expense a thriving limited scale cigar industry could be established in Samoa.

By 1964 the word "expert" was quickly becoming a nasty word to the Samoan people. They were a little tired of people, undoubtedly well meaning, who tried to justify their wages and UN contracts with completely unworkable ideas.

I asked Aggie her opinion of experts. After some consideration, she said she thought the experts now coming to Samoa seemed to be improving rural conditions and were doing good for the country. However, in the earlier days of independence Aggie felt that many of the specialists were inexperienced and often did more harm than good. Certainly in recent years she believed there had been a wonderful improvement.

The first manifestation of spontaneous Samoan public indignation occurred on February 2, 1965, in a demonstration coming from the man in the street, the ordinary worker.

About 500 people marched through Apia to Western Samoa's Parliament House at Mulinu'u to protest to the Government against the high cost of living.

Some marchers carried hastily painted banners and placards calling for higher wages, the re-introduction of the banana bonus, and asked for the remission of recent heavy increases in Customs duty. One banner clearly spelled out their protest reason; "We want to eat".

There was a line-up of many hundreds of spectators along Beach Road on March 2 when about 600 demonstrators marched to Mulinu'u to repeat the protest against the high cost of living. The Samoans were disturbed because their first protest a month before had not been answered by the Government.

At Mulinu'u on the second occasion, about 1,000 members of a body called the Organisation of Peace picketed Parliament. They requested that it consider their petition submitted during the February demonstration protesting against the high cost of living.

There had been parades, processions and demonstrations in the past — during the *Mau* troubles of the twenties and thirties, and during visits of the UN officials in the late forties. But these had all been organised by some sort of authority.

Professor Davidson who played an important part in the formulation of the Samoan Constitution said the protests were a healthy development and happened in most countries. A few months later Government announced a small rise in wages, sufficient however to appease and satisfy the demonstrators.

In the years since Independence in 1962 these demonstrations are the only protests that have been staged. There would be very few countries with such a fine record.

The giant US firm of Potlatch Forests Inc. made a proposition to the Samoan Government, estimating an expenditure of up to £3 million for the first five years. They planned to develop the timber industry on Savai'i, Western Samoa's largest island.

Besides exploiting the timber potential of that island, the investment involved a grandoise scheme for developing power and water supplies for the proposed new town of Asau, hopefully to become the second "city" of Samoa, and for the upgrading of Savai'i roading to facilitate trucking the timber to the Asau wharf.

The investment suggestions followed exhaustive tests made in 1964 in the US by Potlatch on about 26 species of Samoan woods, hard and soft, even as soft as the modelmaking wood, balsa. The American firm proposed building a modern mill in Savai'i capable of handling 50 million super feet of timber annually, and supervising a comprehensive replanting scheme to safeguard the future.

"I believe this is a wonderful opportunity to make a major step forward in economic development aimed at improving the lot of our people," said Prime Minister Mata'afa, who was sold on the scheme.

Not so enthusiastic were the chiefs and villagers on Savai'i. Whether they cultivated or used their timber or not, Samoan land is almost a sacred possession and never handed over lightly for lease or any other purpose.

The negotiations for the Potlatch timber scheme probably took longer than any other ever submitted to the Government. Meetings featuring proposals and counter-proposals had decisions prolonged for so long that only the most patient of representatives could have continued pushing the Potlatch cause in Samoa.

Fortunately this was the demeanour of Tom Shelton, their American representative in Samoa. He had permanent accommodation at Aggie's.

"He stayed in Apia for months on end," Aggie told me, "occasionally returning to America for further talks with the parent company. He most certainly must have been one of the most patient and persistent of any foreign negotiators ever to come to Samoa seeking contracts or doing business with the Government."

Aggie had never seen him angry or depressed although she thought that Mrs. Shelton had a specially steadying influence on Tom.

The new Intercontinental Hotel in American Samoa was expected to be opened in 1966 so Aggie continued her own expansions.

"I expected we would have an increased number of tourists who would wish to visit Apia once they had seen Pago," explained Aggie, "so we went ahead with plans for another double-storey block of units. It was then that we were planning the semi-circle or U-shape appearance, with the swimming pool in the centre. But we didn't know if all our thoughts would ever become actual facts."

*   *   *

Seldom in Samoa are there actual threats of violence and death — it's a peaceful country where there's not even a small army. So it was surprising when numerous reports reaching the police in July, 1965, confirmed that the lives of the Head of State and the Prime Minister were in danger.

It seemed that the Moors brothers were ready to upset the peaceful equilibrium of Apia. Harry and Oliver Moors were sons of prominent politician

Afoafouvale Misimoa. They were born in Western Samoa but both held United States citizenship.

On the morning of July 8 after attending their sister's birthday party the night before, the brothers went to the RSA Club in Beach Road for further drinks.

Witnesses claimed that while drinking in the club Harry and Oliver threatened to kill the Head of State, Prime Minister Mata'afa and certain Europeans, including Auditor-General J. Campagnolo, and Acting Harbourmaster Captain J. Jones.

Before long there were armed guards around the residence of the Head of State (Tanumafili Malietoa) at Vailima, and the Prime Minister's home at Lepea.

Deportation orders against Harry J. Moors and his brother Oliver, were then issued in Apia. The orders remained valid for 10 days and during this period Mata'afa travelled in his car with an armed bodyguard. Armed guards were placed at the houses of the Head of State and the European officials because it was considered the threats still existed.

On July 20 the orders were withdrawn after the Moors brothers had called on the Prime Minister, and, in the words of the *Samoa Bulletin*, had "made their peace with him".

It seems that one of the threatened Europeans, Captain J. W. Jones, had been acting as Harbourmaster in Apia since the dismissal of Captain Harry Moors earlier in the year. On August 5 Jones fell into the sea from the pilot boat as he was about to board the *Thorsisle* to bring it into harbour. He collapsed with a heart attack soon after being helped back on board and was found to be dead on arrival at the hospital.

Overseas investors were envious of the success of Aggie Grey's Hotel and many experts were visiting Samoa. Consultants from Hawaii reported in

November that the first resort hotel should be built at Cape Lefatu, some nine miles beyond the airport at Faleolo and about 30 miles from Apia. Their recommendations were for a 100-room hotel costing £600,000.

Mr. Fred Betham, Samoa's Minister of Finance, told Parliament the Government did not have enough money to finance this project solely, so it was important to induce private capital to invest in it.

He added that the Government was prepared to invest £40,000 in the hotel in 1966, and £60,000 in 1967, and that it was hoped to open the hotel in 1968. These proposals did not worry Aggie. Many similar ideas had been discussed in the past and more were to be wishfully tabled in the near future — to little avail.

* * *

The worst hurricane to rip through the South Seas for seventy-five years devastated Upolu and Savai'i when it struck Samoa on January 29, 30 and 31, in 1966. The hurricane also wreaked havoc in parts of the Cook Group, Wallis and Futuna Islands and the Tokelaus.

The winds, reaching more than 125 miles an hour, tore through the Central Pacific causing hundreds of thousands of dollars worth of damage and the loss of nearly 40 lives.

In Western Samoa the Government sent out appeals for help to New Zealand, Australia, Canada, the United States, the International Red Cross and the United Nations.

Hurricanes in the past had caused heavy damage in certain areas of Samoa, but this one for the first time had devastated the length and breadth of both islands. Ten people died, mostly from falling trees, and the cost to the country was an estimated £3 million in damage and possible loss of earnings over the next year.

The earliest warnings of an approaching tropical storm were issued during the morning of Saturday, January 29. Gale force winds began early in the afternoon and continued until 4 o'clock Sunday morning with a strength averaging about 55 m.p.h. Just over three inches of rain fell during the 24-hour storm. The maximum gust recorded by Apia Observatory was 93 m.p.h., at 8 p.m. on the Saturday.

In Apia, after the storm had passed, Government officials said that the future had many problems. The staple food crop of bananas had been almost destroyed and would not be able to produce fruit again for at least five months. The secondary staple food, breadfruit, was 75% destroyed and authorities predicted a serious food shortage by the end of the next six months.

Some of the villagers were not doing their best to assist in the huge job of clearing the debris caused by the winds. A member of the Prime Minister Mata'afa's Hurricane Relief Committee, formed to co-ordinate and distribute aid, was shocked to find villagers playing cricket wherever he went, and on every day of the week except Sunday. As soon as Mata'afa heard about this laxity he issued a directive forbidding cricket to be played except on Wednesdays and Saturdays.

* * *

Western Samoa's own airline had weathered many turbulent periods and with a new team in charge the company's future seemed quite rosy. Major expansion of services had been decided when tragedy struck Polynesian Airlines.

On May 11, 1966, one of its two DC3 aircraft disintegrated in the air with three crew members on board.

The disaster occurred shortly after 6 p.m. when the aircraft had taken off from Faleolo Airport on a routine training flight. On board were new general manager Captain George Scott, 41, operations manager Captain Jerry Stancil, and co-pilot Alastair Gibbens. Scott and Stancil were Americans and Gibbens was a New Zealander. Stancil was married to a local girl, formerly Anna Wulf, who at the time was pregnant. Gibbens was married with no children.

Early reports stated that Samoan fishermen from Savai'i saw the plane explode in mid-air and fall into the sea. They paddled to the scene of the wreckage and picked up floating pieces of the aircraft. Polynesian Airlines had purchased the crashed DC3 from the United States in 1965 and it was fitted with extended range tanks for the long haul to Raratonga, then part of their regular schedule.

The New Zealand investigators found that the accident was most probably caused by a specially fitted air stair door blowing open, breaking loose and crashing into the tail structure. This door had often given trouble on other occasions, being difficult to close. In fact once previously it had dropped open as the engines were being warmed up before taking off.

I am one of the many who could vouch for that rear door's inefficiency. The DC3 used to leave Nadi at the unearthly hour of 2 a.m. on a scheduled flight to Apia — 3¾ hours in the dark. On one of these early morning flights when I was a sleepy passenger the take-off was delayed — trouble with the rear door.

Down the aisle came George, the Captain, a well-known aviation identity.

"No one else seems to be able to properly close this," he claimed with a grin of satisfaction as he slammed shut the offending door, checked the coloured indicator lights, and hurried back to the flight deck.

When the DC3 crashed into the sea on that ill-fated day in May, 1966, Captain George was on long service leave in the United States.

*　　*　　*

The 25 acre reclamation area on the Apia seafront in 1966 was still bare and dusty, but all this was to change according to Z. M. Wolak, a United Nations expert architect-town planner. Mr. Wolak spent 14 months drawing complete specifications for use of the reclamation even down to the exact position and variety of more than 160 Samoan trees and shrubs. According to Mr. Wolak, the recreational area would consist of playgrounds, lawns, parking spaces with beautiful garden paths featuring Samoan flora, colourful flower gardens, green arcades, reflecting pools, and a mooring point for small boats.

The first stage of the plan would take five years, said Mr. Wolak, and the complete improvements might be extended over a 20-year period.

*　　*　　*

Captain Ron Duffield, general manager of Fiji Airways from 1964 to 1974, was well-known in Pacific aviation circles.

He frequently visited Apia and always stayed at Aggie's. Ron did a remarkable job in transforming an

173

insignificant island airline equipped with obsolete aircraft into the modern and competitive Air Pacific as it is now known.

"When I visited Aggie's, work became a relaxation in an atmosphere of friendliness unsurpassed in the South Seas," Ron told me.

"I delighted in having an evening drink and talking with Aggie. She is a wonderful person and I regard her as one of my best friends. If ever there was a chance when I could repay Aggie's hospitality, I'd always seize the opportunity."

Ron chuckled when he recalled receiving an urgent telegram in Suva from Apia; "We have no butter, please send me two cases, love Aggie."

At the time a shipping strike was preventing supplies of frozen food reaching Western Samoa.

"I immediately asked my secretary to buy the butter and have it sent to Apia. We had a Heron flight that day so urgency was needed," said Ron.

His secretary was worried. "Is it true, Captain, you are going to retire and sell butter in the islands?"

Ron assured her that it was not the case. He would continue to sell seats on aeroplanes. This request for butter was something special for a lady friend in Samoa.

The secretary was still doubtful. "This butter is going to cost a lot of money, Captain. When is this lady friend of yours going to pay?"

"I'll be fully responsible for the cost of the two cases," Ron assured her.

The butter reached Aggie the same day that she sent the telegram. Probably it was delivered to her hotel even quicker than if she had been able to order it from a store in Apia.

*　　*　　*

The first deep sea wharf in Western Samoa was nearing completion towards the end of 1965. Located down past Aggie's at Matautu Point the wharf owed its construction to a £1 million loan by NZ and £500,000 which was raised locally.

*　　*　　*

During 1967 construction commenced on the largest block of units yet added to Aggie's Hotel. This L-shaped extension around the area reserved for the swimming pool was arranged as a matching two-storey building to occupy another 70 guests.

The new addition was to be their most expensive outlay so far, one of tremendous importance in Aggie's dominoe plan. It certainly needed much serious thinking. Would tourists continue to come to Western Samoa? Would their numbers increase? Would they stay at Aggie's Hotel?

These were some of the vital questions to be considered. Many hotels had less than the 40 rooms altogether, yet to Aggie this was but another increase to her already extensive complex.

Faith in herself, her family, and her staff convinced Aggie that despite the considerable financial commitment she should take the risk — and construction began.

Chapter 13

Expansion at Aggie's (1968-1972)

When the latest group of extensions to Aggie's was completed they enclosed the far end of the property in an impressive semi-circle of double storey units. All the rooms had the same modern conveniences as those contructed in the previous three years.

There was a sprinkling of single rooms to cater for the many commercial travellers who visited Apia. These regulars, mainly from New Zealand and Fiji, have always made Aggie's their home in Samoa. Ever anxious to please them, Aggie has the kitchen prepare Indian food — in fact some of the Indians from Suva bring their own favourite curry powders and spices.

Obviously the Government had been taking a close look at Aggie's Hotel with a view to obtaining a bigger share of the tourist dollar. Travelodge Australia had talks with the Government to build a million dollar 100-room motel on the site of the old Casino on Beach Road. Travelodge proposed a joint project involving the demolition of the old DH & PG landmark and the re-location of the seafront road so that the new motel had no passing traffic to distract the view of the sea.

Aggie was not unduly worried about this latest

Aggie with the Prime Minister of
Fiji, Ratu Sir Kamisese Mara

Maggie on her 80th birthday, 29 July, 1973

Aggie with Raymond Burr, television personality

Aggie, Marina and staff
(Photo courtesy James Siers, author of "Samoa in Color")

Aggie, circa 1970

Aggie at her 8oth birthday party, 31 October, 1977 *(Gary Fearnley)*

Aggie's grandchilden Tanya and Frederick with their pet dog,
31 October, 1977 *(Gary Fearnley)*

Daughter-in-law Marina and staff at the *fiafia*, 31 October, 1977 *(Gary Fearnley*

Aggie's Hotel swimming pool and units

Customs House, Apia, 1906

Beach Road, Apia, 1906

The *Mau* bandstand office, on the road to the airport

Wreck of the *Adler* from the 1889 hurricane.
Now covered by the reclamation adjacent Beach Road.
Taken in 1960

IA SAMOA UMA.

Ua tatela ma ua toe faafo'i e Nelesoni lana tagi na fai'a e faasaga i le Fai Nusipepa "Herald", ma o le a ia totogi atu i le Fai Nusipepa o le totogi o mea uma ua alu talu lana mea na fai.

O Molimau na valaauina ua toe foi mai i Samoa.

O le uiga o lenei mea a faapea :—

1. Ua faai'uina le Su'ega ma ua i'u nei lava.

2. O tupe sa lafo ma totogi atu e le Mau ua faamaumauina lava i le tautiga le aogā.

3. Ua toe 'olegia foi le Mau i folafolaga sese.

10. Fepuari 1930.

S. S. ALLEN,

KOVANA.

TRANSLATION—

TO ALL SAMOA

Nelson has withdrawn his action that was filed against the Newspaper "Herald", and he shall pay to the Newspaper all expenses incurred from what he has done.

Witnesses summoned have returned to Samoa.

This means:—

1. The case is closed forthwith.
2. The monies that were subscribed by the Mau have been wasted in a useless campaign.
3. The Mau is further deceived by false promises.

10 February 1930

S. S. ALLEN,
GOVERNOR

"Surrender" leaflet dropped by a New Zealand seaplane during the
Mau troubles, 1930

Some of Aggie's family at her 75th birthday.
From left: Mrs. Maureen Hannan, Edward Grey, Aggie,
Gordon Hay-Mackenzie, Mrs. Pele Turner, 31 October, 1972

Front of Aggie's Hotel, 1960   Town Clock, Beach Road, Apia, 1

Vailima, Robert Louis Stevenson's home, taken in 1960 when it was the residence of the New Zealand High Commissioner

Beach Road in 1960. Burns Philp in foreground, Chief Post Office, Bank of Western Samoa and Methodist Church

threat to her monopoly of the tourist trade. In the twenty years since the end of World War II she had increased her guest accommodation from 20 in the days of the original International Hotel building to a total of 120 in 1968. Aggie probably knew that any outsider would encounter untold difficulties setting up against her in the hotel business.

Perhaps Travelodge, as big as they are, sensed these problems because with patience apparently exhausted, they bowed out. The reason given for their change of heart was that the Government would not agree to re-routing the seafront road.

The Samoan language, like many other that served "primitive" communities, needed some adoptions to be fully understood with the complexities of foreign words. It was inevitable that Samoa had to take words from the language of other countries with whom it had contact. A short-term visitor will probably not hear any of these examples of Samoanisation.

There is always considerable amusement to be had with the waiters at Aggie's if a tourist drops a few interesting requests at the dinner table. For instance butter is *pata*, knife is *naifi*, bread is *falaoa*, sugar is *suka*, milk is *susu*. But you must be careful when framing your order for milk because *susu* has a double meaning.

The borrowed word most frequently used must be *pisupo*. In the early days, when the first shipment of miraculous food arrived in cans, it so happened that it comprised only pea soup. A Samoan word had to be given to the foreign import and this was *pisupo*, simply pronounced pea-soupo.

As time passed, various other foodstuffs arrived in cans — all to be called *pisupo*, no matter what their contents. The Samoans didn't particularly like pea soup, in fact there were very few varieties of canned foods that did appeal to their palate.

The exception was corned beef from New Zealand. It swept Samoa like wildfire. Everybody liked this new *pisupo* and the name has stuck with it ever since. The almost fanatic love of *pisupo* by Samoans resulted in the commodity in earlier days being commercially supplied in kegs weighing up to 100 pounds.

Guests at Aggie's always have an opportunity at a *fiafia* to sample Samoan foods. Whether *pisupo* can be classed as typically Samoan is perhaps uncertain, but this delicacy is always on the menu.

I asked Aggie about her recipes for *pisupo*.

"Cut up an onion, add a dash of water, and boil, then add to the mixture the *pisupo*. Other ingredients can be Chinese cabbage and watercress; but always have an onion in the mixture.

"*Pisupo* should be well turned in the cooking so that it mixes thoroughly with the onions or the cabbage and watercress. Pepper may be added but no salt until the mixture is tasted."

Aggie thought a delicious way of serving *pisupo* is fried. "First I fry an onion in butter and add some flour. After a few minutes add the *pisupo* and a little water. Mix well and continue to fry until ready to serve. This is my favourite way of preparing *pisupo*."

Pisupo has always been served at Aggie's, even when Prime Minister Mata'afa banned its importation from NZ in 1968. Mata'afa did this in protest at the producers' increased prices of their staple. For a while *pisupo* was off the shelves of the Apia stores, or rather under the counter. There was even a blackmarket in operation — supplies were being smuggled in from American Samoa.

The average Samoan is a big buyer of NZ mutton flaps. This part of the sheep is not eaten in NZ but tons are regularly shipped to the South Sea islands, especially Tonga, Fiji and Samoa. Selling at 15 cents a pound in 1968, mutton flaps were the cheapest meat available to Samoans.

"Mutton flaps are still the cheapest meat that can be purchased in Samoa," said Aggie. "In the villages the meat is cooked by throwing the mutton flaps on to very hot stones of the earth oven. Onion is usually added, and when the two are sizzling they emit a really appetising odour. Sometimes the flaps are wrapped in banana leaves and cooked on the hot stones of the earth oven."

*   *   *

During mid-1968 Prime Minister Mata'afa, holding the portfolio of Minister of Police, was considering a parliamentary bill aimed at complete prohibition. Reasons suggested by locals were that religious pressure had been brought to bear on the Prime Minister.

Really speaking, Western Samoa even then, by law, was a dry country. Liquor was still completely prohibited to Samoans by a 1921 Act. This ruling made anyone manufacturing, importing, or selling intoxicating liquor liable to a fine of $400 or one year's imprisonment. Actually, however, liquor was freely available at the many clubs to Samoans and Europeans alike.

"By 1968 I did not have any liquor supply problems despite the technicality in the law that we were still a dry country," Aggie told me. "I guess that law had been in existence so long that no-one wished to be the first to suggest it should be abolished."

Western Samoa's second deep sea wharf at Asau on the island of Savai'i had been completed in 1966.

The million dollar Asau wharf was a case of putting the cart before the horse. The wharf was ready to be used before the discovery was made that the coral or volcanic seabed was too tough to dredge to the depth required to accommodate ocean-going liners.

The NZ Navy was occupied for a year exploding hundreds of tons of war surplus bombs and TNT in a vain attempt to complete the 3,600 ft. channel through the lagoon to the open sea.

Many people have wondered why the expensive wharf was built in faraway Asau when the money used could well have been spent providing larger and better facilities for shipping in Apia. Frequently it has been said that the Asau construction was linked with the Potlatch Timber project on Savai'i. However this is incorrect because the wharf was planned long before the American firm made its first approaches with logging proposals.

When the wharf proposals for Apia were being discussed in Parliament there was a certain amount of opposition from the members representing Savai'i. It did appear that although opinion was unanimous that the Apia construction was urgently needed, the MPs from Savai'i would not give their support unless Savai'i also got a wharf.

The Asau wharf facility must have played a big part later in the negotiations with Potlatch. Here was an outlet for their timber shipments so their mill should be constructed nearby. When Potlatch signed their agreement on March 19, 1968, neither they nor the Government knew that during the next ten years the wharf would never become navigable to the average ocean-going ship.

During the three years of negotiations in Apia, Tom Shelton had quietly and patiently argued the Potlatch case. The time taken to reach a final agreement must be a record in any country. The firm had a history of sixty years operation in the US and this was one of their few ventures overseas.

For the Samoans it was a big deal — in fact there has never been anything else discussed on such a large scale. They were certainly entitled to study very closely the proposals and to completely protect their people to the best of their ability.

The contract was initially for forty years with Samoa receiving 25 per cent of the net profits from the lumber for the first ten years of operation. At the beginning it was expected that there would be employment at the mills for 14 US personnel and 125 Samoans.

*   *   *

Visitors to Apia in the first six months of 1968 showed an increase of 8.4 per cent over the same period in 1967. A total of 3,972 tourists included 1,662 from the US, an increase of 38 per cent.

Aggie was most encouraged with this news but still regarded dubiously the predictions of travel consultants that by 1970 there would be 20,000 annually coming to Samoa.

The next major projects at Aggie's were the construction of a swimming pool and the giant-sized guest *fale*. To meet demands of tour operators and satisfy the needs of the more sophisticated European and American tourists a swimming pool, the equal of those at Fijian resorts, became a necessity.

Without the modern equipment needed for excavations the initial work was very difficult. Rain seemed always to come at the wrong time, halting the digging and filling the hole with water so deep that for days on end work was at a standstill. By the end of

1968 the excavations were practically completed. Regular guests anxiously awaited completion of the pool, and tour party people expressed disappointment that they had been destined to come too soon to Aggie's.

The remarkable Samoan style *fale* adjacent to the swimming pool was built in 1968. It is here that the *fiafia* and the movie shows are held. Although there is seating for 200, any overflow can be accommodated on the lawns and around the pool, which was completed in 1969.

Coming from Honolulu to Apia tourists find a tremendous contrast in style of food and surroundings, but most of all in the friendly carefree approach to life by the Samoans.

Statistics on tourist influx must have convinced Pan American Airways that for the eight years from 1960 to 1968 Polynesian Airlines had profited very well with their monopoly of the Pago-Apia route. The Americans then proposed to start a twice-daily service using 40-seater Fokker Friendships.

Pan Am Pacific manager W. Mullahey enthusiastically told travel agents in Apia, "This is the biggest thing to have happened to Western Samoa since independence. The country will need another 300-500 hotel rooms."

Polynesian Airlines opposed the move, saying there was insufficient traffic for two airlines and that the service would not operate. They were right — the Western Samoan Government was able to block the proposal, but the deferment wasn't as easy as in 1960. It was obvious that before many years reciprocal rights would have to be granted.

The air link between the two Samoas was the lifeline of tourism for Aggie. For the fulfilment of contracts and the even flow of visitors the route needed a thoroughly reliable operator. Polynesian Airlines was having a run of bad luck — in the preceding two years they, too, had suffered at the hands of "experts".

The company had foolishly chartered a DC4 from an American firm — the Charlotte Aircraft Corporation of North Carolina. The aircraft was continually a source of trouble right from the beginning of the lease when it had to go to NZ for an airworthiness certificate.

Unfortunately there had never been a DC4 under the NZ Department of Civil Aviation. Even when operating in Samoa, the aeroplane was grounded more often than it was flying.

The DC4 became an item of South Seas history when in mid-August, 1969, it was probably the first aircraft ever to be "arrested". Captain Jim Cole had made his scheduled flight to Pago. Not very long after landing a representative of Charlotte Aircraft Corporation chained the landing wheels and removed some vital parts from the DC4. As a result of a court case in Los Angeles the jinxed plane went back to America in early September.

As Polynesian Airlines now had only a single DC3 in its fleet the company chartered a Fiji Airways HS748 to fly the Apia-Tonga and Apia-Fiji routes. It was forced to rely on the DC3 for the twice daily service to Pago.

* * *

There had been an increasing number of German tourist parties passing through Samoa, spending the usual three days there and then going on to Pago Pago or Tonga or Fiji.

Sunday is essentially a religious day in Samoa but

visitors had to make the most of their limited stay. One particular Sunday a party of Germans were touring through the nearby villages of Apia, all armed with cameras and endeavouring to catch the local scene and customs of the people as much as possible during their 72 hours.

The party pulled up in front of the village of Lepea which was the home of the Prime Minister. Some of the party stayed on the roadway and observed the necessary courtesy they understood to be the local custom for a Sunday. Unfortunately the remainder strolled across the grass towards the *fale* of the Prime Minister, who made an appearance and politely, but firmly, informed them that they should leave the area. The Germans took very little notice, maybe because they could not understand or perhaps they didn't wish to comprehend. Possibly they considered that they should take a chance as this opportunity to photograph a Prime Minister might never happen again.

The Prime Minister, a very well educated person, was generally tactful with foreigners but on this occasion his patience was exhausted.

One ardent camera fan continued to painstakingly shoot scenes of the Prime Minister and villagers in the vicinity. Mata'afa immediately grabbed the tourist by his shirt collar, shook him like a wet blanket, and completed the treatment with a solid Samoan punch which quickly brought blood to the nose of the German tourist. Without a doubt this forthright action quickly dispersed the party of persistent cameramen who took off as fast as their heavily laden camera bags permitted.

Of course they came back to the hotel and voiced their opinion at the way they had been treated — they were tourists coming to Samoa willing to spend large sums of money and this unseemly reception!

When informed of the incident by the tourists Aggie was furious and left immediately for Lepea to take up the matter with Mata'afa. Obviously the much maligned Apia telephone service was working efficiently that Sunday afternoon because when she arrived at his village she found the Prime Minister had been tipped off and was missing. So was his four-wheel-drive jeep, which was then taking him on an urgent visit to the other end of the island, with tracks impassable for ordinary cars such as Aggie's.

When questioned about the incident Mata'afa confirmed he did strike a German tourist trespassing on the Lepea *malae* on Sunday.

"I slapped his face because he kept taking my picture," said the Prime Minister. "It was the bus driver I was really annoyed with because all local tour agents know that Lepea is off limits to tourists at all times, not only just on Sundays."

Very soon a notice appeared in hotels stating that all tourist parties were instructed to observe the customs of the Samoans, emphasising quite truly that the tourists were guests of the country and that it was up to them to do the right thing and not offend. The drivers and guides on the tourist buses were to be held responsible for the actions of their charges, for after all they were Samoans and should know the customs of their country.

Opening new buildings such as churches, mission houses, traders' stores, roads, bridges, schools and post offices is always an event of considerable importance to Samoans. Each function calls for suitable speeches, much dancing, singing and feasting, and of course a *kava* ceremony if the guests are of sufficiently high standing.

If the occasion is of national significance, like a new

church or a post office, it attracts bus-loads of fun-seeking people from many districts. They come with new songs to sing, new dances, and gifts of money.

The amount of *tala* and *sene* each family subscribes on these occasions will at appropriate intervals throughout the ceremony be loudly proclaimed on behalf of the recipient to the poker-faced assembly. Those who have given the most will feel pleased with themselves; those who have not shown sufficient generosity may feel ashamed — and hasten to show more respect by increasing their monetary contribution immediately or making a promise to do so.

A typical ceremony took place when the post office at the village of Malaemalu was opened for business on October 1, 1971.

On this special occasion the ceremony was conducted by the Minister of the Post Office, Fuimaono Moasope. As the Post Office at Malaemalu was in the constituency of the Minister, a full ceremony involving *kava* was enacted by the chiefs and orators of the village. On an occasion such as this the Director of the Post Office always accompanies the Minister. Also in the party was a talking chief or orator representing the Post Office headquarters. He, too, was a high chief in his own village.

When the chiefs and the visitors were seated cross-legged in the *fale* with their backs against poles, the chiefs decided who would be their actual spokesman for this important function. When a decision was reached the selected chief began his speech. This was followed by a response from the spokesman for the Post Office. Then there was a cross exchange of a friendly, complimentary, and welcoming nature lasting for maybe the next half hour. The Minister for the Post Office made a speech, received by the chiefs and orators with courtesy and acclaim.

186

During the speeches a *taupou* of the village, a girl who will mix the *kava*, had appeared and was seated cross-legged in the *fale* with a *kava* bowl in front of her. A ceremonial *kava* root was presented to each of the distinguished visitors and the roots lay in front of each of the guests during the speeches. These roots were removed and placed out of the way once the *kava* ceremony itself began. The *kava* cermony commenced when a chief took a half-coconut shell containing *kava*, and with a flourish and several turns in the middle of the *fale*, presented it to the most distinguished visitor, in this case the Minister for the Post Office. The Minister dropped a few portions of the *kava* onto the mat in front of him, drank from the bowl and then tipped the liquid out.

Next the *kava* was presented to a chief of the village and he drank from it, then tipped away the remainder. This procedure continued until all the visitors and a number of chiefs had been given *kava* to drink. The final cup went to the head of the village who earlier had been selected as their spokesman. Therefore the first and last drinks at the *kava* ceremony go to the two highest ranking people present at that particular function.

When the *kava* ceremony was completed, food was brought in and presented to the Minister and to the Director, followed by the presentation of a fine mat to each of them. These special gifts were then taken away and the food was brought in by the women of the village who had been preparing it during the morning. A supply of food was placed in front of every person, visitors and chiefs of the village alike. Meanwhile some of the girls sat down beside the guests intent on fanning both the food and the visitors to keep away the flies. The food, a mixture of European and local Samoan dishes, included such things as fish, *taro*, *pisupo*, *palusami*, chow mein, and that greatest of Samoan delicacies, wild pigeon.

Just before the ceremony in the *fale* finished the Minister for the Post Office presented a sum of money to the village. In this case it was 25 *tala* in appreciation of their kindness and generosity in providing food and arranging the *kava* ceremony.

After the meal, bowls were provided for washing of hands and the party proceeded to the Post Office where the Minister cut the ribbon to open the building. Chiefs, orators and other members of the village inspected the Post Office, praising this new and important addition which would greatly enhance their status.

*   *   *

Polynesian Airlines received a major setback when the only DC3 they owned crashed shortly after a 3 a.m. take-off at Faleolo on January 13, 1970. Everyone aboard the aircraft was killed, 29 passengers including eight children and the crew of three, when the plane dived into the sea near the end of the airstrip.

At this time Polynesian Airlines only other DC3 was leased and the HS748 was chartered from Fiji Airways who were then managing the Samoan airline.

An official enquiry found that at the time of take-off the aircraft had flown head-on into a violent squall. The intensity of this turbulence had caused the pilot to lose control at a critical time.

Polynesian Airlines, who had greatly improved their services to the air traveller, suffered severely as a result of the crash. Undoubtedly it was the most tragic episode in their ten-year history — up until

1970 there had been only one worse crash in the South Pacific. That was the 1948 disaster at Lae, New Guinea, when 37 people lost their lives.

The tourist trade in Apia was not being helped by the uncertainty that existed for visitors arriving and departing. Government's attitude towards a possible tourist bonanza was that they wished to have a "controlled" influx.

Aggie thought this plan had merits.

"Their idea is good in many ways," she explained, "but just how do you control the flow of people? Certainly we do not want Western Samoa to lose its unique identity and age-old traditions. These are the wonderful assets we have to offer the world.

"But how can a control operate? If a tour operator wants to send us 1,000 people in a certain period, do we have to say that only 500 can come?"

Although Western Samoa had been independent since 1962 it was not until mid-1970 that Prime Minister Tupua Tamasese Lealofi announced that the nation would join the British Commonwealth.

"It was a good move," said Aggie, "because our country had received a lot of assistance especially with education, although we didn't do what is usual and join the Commonwealth immediately after independence."

Samoa's leaders have always been cautious in international matters since they had their own control. Although they joined the Commonwealth in 1970 Samoa was not yet a member of UN.

There had been an almost continuous plea from the tourist trade in Apia to upgrade the Faleolo airport. So it was good news for the economy of the country when the announcement was made that a US $3.1 million airport would be built capable of handling BAC111 jets and probably Boeing 737s.

A new modern terminal building was included in the project which was expected to be finished by June, 1972. The existing runway was to be used while the new 7,300 ft. strip, with 5,500 ft. sealed was built alongside.

The use of jets was welcomed because it meant faster flights to Fiji and more tourists to fill the hotel rooms. Aggie decided it was time then to further increase the occupancy of her hotel. Plans were drawn up for a block which would have the hotel laundry on ground level and eight rooms upstairs.

*   *   *

Samoa was visited by another international raft when *La Balsa* on a voyage from Ecuador to Australia drifted near Asau. The four men and a cat had left on May 29, 1970, intent on proving that such a journey was possible on a raft built along the same lines as those constructed by early South American Indians.

When the crew sighted Samoa it was the first land they had seen since passing the Galapagos Islands three months earlier. They welcomed the offer of fruit and supplies when a launch was prepared to tow them into Sataua Bay. The raftsmen were impressed and enjoyed Samoa so much that they stayed until September 14 instead of immediately sailing away as they intended.

When *La Balsa* reached Australia on November 6, 1970, they received a tumultuous welcome. Only once during the long voyage did the crew set foot on land and that was on Samoa.

Different types of research vessels of many nations have called at Samoa from time to time and always they were made welcome, even though sometimes the reasons given for study were questionable. During

February, 1971, a Japanese vessel, the *Kaiyo Maru*, brought scientists from various parts of the world.

Exploration seemed to be going very well for although the ship was anchored in the harbour a launch was readily available.

Late one afternoon a Japanese scientist, Mr. Yoshikazu Saito, came ashore, and was never seen again. He simply vanished into thin air. If he had been swimming his body was not washed up to shore. Perhaps he could have been taken by a shark, but sharks are not often seen inside the reef. The disappearance was completely mystifying. Locals commented that if he had drowned then certainly his body should have been washed ashore.

The captain of the *Kaiyo Maru* decided he would postpone his departure and stay in Apia until some definite trace was found of Saito. The police advertised the matter widely but still no trace could be found of the missing Japanese. About a week after the disappearance the scientist's father and brother arrived from Tokyo to stay at Aggie's.

"It was quite a sensation for several weeks," said Aggie, "especially when the family of the scientist advertised a large reward would be paid — I think it was one thousand *tala* — for information leading to the recovery of their missing relative.

"Samoans normally will not keep a secret such as this. We thought maybe the Japanese was murdered for money. But had this been the case somebody would have known about it. The body would have to be buried. But no, he simply vanished."

The relatives stayed for more than a week at Aggie's hoping that some traces could be found. Then they said they regretted they must return to Japan. At the same time the research vessel sailed out of Samoa, less one member of her scientific crew.

At the coroner's inquest 16 months later it was disclosed that a handbag, watch, belt, and butterfly net had been found at Lauii beach and handed to the police. The *Samoa Times* reported that "there had been police suspicion of foul play. Mr. Spring said in his verdict that Mr. Saito had died while at sea".

During 1971 many clubs were opened not only in the centre of Apia but also in the residential areas. A Samoan club is quite different to clubs in the Western world. Perhaps they could be likened to taverns but could be simply described as rooms or larger areas where liquor is obtainable, a loudspeaker pounds out distorted music, and girls are available as dancing partners.

At that time it appeared an easy matter to open a club — find some space and buy your supply of beer and spirits from the Government bond store, and you were in business.

The police had received complaints from residents that some clubs stayed open until 4 a.m. Behaviour and noise was described as most objectionable so the authorities ruled that clubs would be licensed to operate only until midnight.

One criticism was that the ruling would offend tourists who wished to continue after 12 o'clock. The new regulation did not affect Aggie as she emphasised "entertainment at my hotel finishes at a respectable hour. The bar is usually closed at 10 p.m. so that guests may always have a good night's sleep."

In April, 1971, the Fiji hotel operators, Naviti Investments, were reported to be forming a company linked with the Western Samoa Government to build a 100-room hotel on the Casino site on Beach Road. This was the location that interested Travelodge for several years but negotiations lapsed.

During August in the same year statistics were

released showing a 29 per cent increase in visitors during the first four months of 1971 compared with the same period in 1970.

This news must have encouraged a group of investors to enquire about the feasibility of erecting a cable car to run to Stevenson's tomb on the summit of Mt. Vaea. They were all local residents who were capable of assessing whether the proposal would be worth serious consideration. Probably the group made some comparisons with the cable car that had been operating in Pago for a number of years.

The lower level terminal for the Mt. Vaea car was planned to be near Vailima, official residence of the Head of State. Perhaps the possibility of a flood of cable car tourists and the resultant traffic around the old home of Stevenson was one of the reasons why the scheme did not get off the ground.

I asked Aggie what she thought about the cable car proposals. She said: "Yes, it was a good idea and the promoters had gone into it quite carefully. Raising the finance and some other Government problems seemed to be the reason why it was not proceeded with. But in any case it is much more interesting nowadays for tourists to walk up Mt. Vaea to the grave since the pathway has been improved."

As 1971 drew to a close, one of Samoa's most prominent and respected citizens died. Eugene Friedrich Paul, OBE, passed away in Honolulu on December 28, following a spinal operation. Eugene Paul, who was 71, had been engaged in almost every facet of trading in Western Samoa. He was specially involved in the transport business on the land, sea and air.

In 1926 he founded Gold Star Transport Company which later incorporated taxis. For many years the only reliable cabs in Apia were Gold Star — always a little more expensive but well worth the difference.

Eugene Paul was one who thoroughly agreed with Aggie in the need to have an air link between Pago and Apia. Right from the preliminary Polynesian Airlines meetings in 1959 he used every endeavour to overcome the seemingly unending problems. Eugene Paul knew little about running an airline at that time but he learned the hard way. Elected chairman of Polynesian Airlines in 1960 he still held that position at the time of his death.

Aggie spoke about Eugene Paul, who she thought had been one of the most successful business people in modern Apia.

"Eugene Paul began with one old car," said Aggie, "and from this one vehicle he progressed to the big transport company which exists today — Gold Star, who operate buses in Apia and all over the country."

By mid-1971 the Potlatch timber mill was in operation following the overcoming of numerous obstacles which had caused expensive delays. The American firm had expected to use the Asau wharf not only to export their sawn timber, but also to discharge all their mill construction equipment arriving from overseas.

Instead of this convenient arrangement everything had to be barged from Apia to Asau, a most expensive and time-consuming operation. Asau was still a wharf without ships, a monument to unlimited funds but too limited thought.

A Tongan ship, the *Niuvakai*, was able to berth at the wharf, and did make a number of voyages to the US and elsewhere for Potlatch. As far as most other ships were concerned the harbour pilots refused to accept responsibility of navigating through the channel because of the lack of clearance above the volcanic sea floor even at highest tide.

There seemed no limit to the flow of money-making proposals aimed at a share of the tourist earnings. A licence was granted to Mr. Tusi Taualii to operate a hovercraft between the ferry departure wharf at Mulifanua and Salelologa on Savai'i. The hovercraft was expected by the end of 1971 but the service did not eventuate.

There was a strong rumour that the Canadian Government was involved in a plan to build a hotel on top of Mt. Vaea. After an official denial in Apia little further was heard of this scheme.

In 1971 Polynesian Airlines had inspected both Fokker and HS748 aircraft with a view to purchasing their own plane. The Government had earlier named PAL as the national flag carrier of Western Samoa.

When it appeared there were financial problems in the way of the purchase of a new aircraft the Government stepped in and virtually nationalised the airline. As holders of 51 per cent of the shares the Government was able to guarantee the new aircraft, an HS748, which arrived towards the end of January, 1972, the first modern plane PAL had ever owned.

Then the Minister of Civil Aviation, Tupuola Efi, explained the reasons for Government involvement saying, "In a state as small and isolated as ours with an increasing requirement for travel to our island neighbours and other countries and with an increasing flow of visitors from abroad, it is essential that Government should have some control over, and play a significant role in, the instrument of airline responsibility for providing the communication."

Alan Grey was appointed a director of Polynesian Airlines. With such a close involvement in tourism it was fitting that Alan was made a board member.

Pan Am rethought their plans to acquire the reciprocal rights for the Pago-Apia route. As Fokkers had earlier been blocked effectively by the Western Samoa Government, the airline now proposed using light aircraft.

In this 1972 move Pan Am suggested they operate a type of shuttle service between the two Samoas. There were several light planes available such as those belonging to Air Samoa, and these, they said, would be chartered. Pan Am reasoned that if the 40-seater Fokkers were considered a threat to Polynesian Airlines then surely these light aircraft could not be harmful and must be acceptable.

By no means over-confident the Americans anxiously awaited the Government's answer. On this occasion Minister of Civil Aviation, Tupuola Efi, again effectively "blocked" the Pan Am light aircraft application.

Then in a masterly show of diplomacy the Minister said that in maybe three to five years the expected heavy traffic on the route would require Pan Am's larger aircraft.

According to *Samoa Times* Tupuola Efi, in his most encouraging manner, told the Americans: "When the time comes we will not merely be asking you to come, we will be screaming for you to come."

There was further good news to follow for PAL — and for Western Samoa. For the second year running, board chairman Ted Annandale announced the airline was operating profitably. It wasn't a big profit, but it was a profit and that was the important thing. Certainly it was happy news for the tourist industry — more people were travelling.

It was about this time that Aggie made a decision to again enlarge the hotel by building an L-shaped double-storey block of units at the rear of Alan and Marina's house. By joining the proposed building to the existing structure the effect would be to form another U-shaped complex somewhat smaller than that which surrounded the new swimming pool.

Provided everything went to schedule the new block would be ready for occupation during 1973. It would add accommodation for another 50 guests, making Aggie's one of the largest hotels in the South Pacific area.

If not the largest then it was by far the best-known and most popular of any of the hotels in the South Seas. Unsurpassed for friendliness it had Aggie as a figurehead — Aggie, who had suffered countless set-backs, yet had never lost her unique sense of humour, her old-world charm. Aggie had won through. Now she was an unqualified success — it was 30 years since she had sold hamburgers on Beach Road.

When the tourism stamps were issued for Western Samoa in August, 1971, one of them showed Aggie Grey and her hotel. Aggie did not know this stamp was going to appear as her son, Alan, had kept it a secret. Alan had seen the artwork and agreed it was satisfactory because at this time Aggie was in New Zealand.

Aggie's first news of the stamp was when somebody bought a copy of the *Pacific Island Monthly* and showed her the report, which amongst other things, mentioned this was one of the few occasions when a living person, other than Royalty, has been depicted on a postage stamp.

This statement apparently had Aggie worried because she said, "Well I don't feel too well at the present time. I certainly hope I don't die before this stamp can be issued, because then it won't be showing a living person. Maybe I should call Eddie Williams (Director of the Post Office) and see if they can put forward the issue just in case something does happen to me."

197

However nothing happened to Aggie and when the stamp came out as scheduled Aggie was still well alive and active. Many first day envelopes bearing the set of the four stamps publicising Western Samoa tourism were autographed by Aggie. Today these collectors' pieces are in keen demand by philatelists.

Chapter 14

Aggie's After Forty Years
(1973-1979)

In the six years from 1973 to 1979 there was a tremendous change in the lifestyle of the urban areas of Apia. Despite endeavours to limit and maintain the "controlled tourism", more and more people were finding their way to Western Samoa.

Hawaii was overcrowded. There was very little for the tourist in American Samoa. New Zealanders and Australians had seen Fiji, but Western Samoa — well it has always been off the beaten track.

Slowly and surely a visit to the heart of Polynesia was being made easier for the package deal tourist. The great advance on air travel was the introduction of direct Apia-Auckland flights in February, 1978, by Air New Zealand and Polynesian Airlines, using Boeing 737 aircraft.

During 1973 the units begun a year earlier at Aggie's were completed. This addition fitted admirably into the already existing double-storey complex surrounded by lush tropical gardens. The new rooms were to be the last major construction for Aggie's.

The hotel was then able to accommodate 200 guests in what seemed incredible comfort to a few regular travellers who had stayed at Aggie's during the previous twenty-five years. Gone were the stable-like bedrooms from the top floor of the main building — the old International Hotel. Even this area was modernised, separate rooms with airconditioning and all the latest conveniences.

Aggie and her family had decided that the hotel was as large as they could manage and happily control in their customary homely way. They reasoned that there could be no pleasure in owning a giant complex twice the size where guests lost their names and became only a room number.

So extensions stopped and Aggie settled down to enjoy the fruits of nearly forty years hard work. Although she makes her regular trips each year to New Zealand, Aggie always comes back to Samoa.

"I'll never leave these islands," she said to me. "I was born here. This is my home and I shall die here with my people. I have lived a full life, and I'm happy here with my family, especially the grandchildren."

Aggie has always been known for her unlimited generosity. Every deserving cause or charitable institution can be assured of a sympathetic hearing. Seldom does anyone go away empty-handed.

When the Samoan Athletic Association was having problems raising finance for the Commonwealth Games in 1974 Aggie came to their aid with probably the largest individual donation.

She has never forgotten the people of Toamua village — her village. Always Aggie has employed the young people from Toamua at her hotel. When there are special functions at the village, the bestowing of titles, weddings, or funerals, the three daughters of Pele — Maggie, Aggie and Mary — can be counted on to contribute generously.

Aggie has a special interest in the Shriners Hospital located in Hawaii. It is here that much beneficial treatment can be given to crippled children. Her contributions have made possible the admission to the institution of many young Samoans who otherwise would have been disabled for life. Probably this particularly worthy cause is today one of Aggie's greatest charitable interests.

There have been, as mentioned earlier, so many important happenings in the six years to 1979, especially where tourism, hotels and aviation are concerned.

In 1973 Polynesian Airlines' fear of Pan Am involvement on the Apia-Pago route was again dispelled following a successful visit by Western Samoa's Minister of Civil Aviation, Tupuola Efi, to Washington, DC. During discussions when he presented Polynesian's case, Tupuola was able to convince the American civil aviation that Pan Am's competitive entry should be delayed for at least another year.

In the 1970s there was no shortage of applicants to build giant luxury hotels in Samoa. Each promoter seemed intent on surpassing any previous colossal schemes put before the Goverment.

Plans for an ultra-luxury hotel to be erected near Apia were announced late in 1972. To be known as the Royal Samoan Hotel the building was to be erected on a reclaimed land area of some sixty-five acres. It was reported that the first 150 rooms would be completed by the end of the year and a further 300 additional rooms were planned for the future. Other reports said the first stage of the construction was to be a 100-room hotel at a cost of $1.5 million and that the Western Samoan Government was prepared to give a 60-year lease of the land, plus a further 20 years, if the consortium was able to increase the size of the complex to 250 rooms within the first 20 years of occupation. By then it would represent a US $15 million investment.

Reclamation certainly began and houses for construction employees were erected. Rumours were current when, after some months, work on the site suddenly ceased.

Aggie thought that Richard Hadley, the Seattle, USA, multi-millionaire, who was building the hotel was dismayed at the non-fulfilment of certain promised undertakings discussed with the Government.

Aggie said: "I have heard that Hadley expected the international airport at Faleolo would be upgraded so Jumbo jets could land. These aircraft would be able to bring sufficient tourists to make the Royal Samoan Hotel a paying proposition."

At the end of 1978 the building of the hotel had not commenced, neither had provision been made for Jumbo jets to land in Western Samoa.

"An hotel like Hadley's would not have worried us," Aggie considered, "because these tourists would be in the top luxury bracket, people who would be prepared to pay up to $100 a day. My hotel is operated in a different way.

"I want everyone who stays with me to feel this is their home. That's why my meals are served family style, and why all the Samoans who work in my hotel treat the guests just as they would someone in their own homes."

*   *   *

In this story of Samoa it is inevitable that the subject of the rising of the *palolo* must be described. A phenomenon of the South Seas, the *palolo* is a coral sea-worm that surfaces from the crevices of the coral reefs surrounding Upolu and Savai'i.

The mysterious dawn rising which always happens once a year and sometimes twice, during October and November, is controlled by the phases of the moon. Occasionally there is a false alarm because the *palolo* may appear on either the eighth or ninth day after the full moon.

Long before daybreak on the expected morning the villagers are ready with nets, saucepans, or any type of container that will hold the lengths of bubbly sea-worm as it reaches the surface.

"*Palolo* is a great delicacy," according to Aggie, "I'll always buy as much as possible from the villagers. It's the caviare of Samoa, and when cooked looks much the same."

The sea-worm can be kept in refrigerators and enjoyed for months after the rising. There's been many a guest at Aggie's who would have mistaken *palolo* for caviare.

The rising is not confined to Samoa. It occurs in many parts of the South Seas. In Fiji and Tonga it is called *balolo*.

When the *palolo* rises Aggie is usually seen at dawn in her favourite chair underneath her store next door to the hotel. Aggie pays a little more than the regular market price so that her family and the guests may sample the Samoan caviare fresh from the sea.

When cooked, *palolo* can be eaten with boiled eggs, served on toast or on savoury biscuits.

*   *   *

The 1973 elections returned to power as Prime Minister, Fiame Mata'afa Faumuina Mulinu'u. Mata'afa had been unseated as PM in 1970 by Tupua Tamasese Lealofi. Tamasese was given the appointment of Minister for Justice in the new cabinet.

Although Mata'afa received more than half the votes for PM, there was some surprise when it was learned that Tupuola Efi, the outgoing Minister of Civil Aviation, polled very well for the post of PM. The voting was Mata'afa 23, Tupuola 13, and Tamasese 9.

*   *   *

The well-known landmark, the Casino, was finally demolished in 1973. Built in the German days, the timber-framed building was to make way for the Tusitala Hotel, a joint venture by the Government and a Fijian hotel syndicate. The Casino, built in 1910 as a lodging house for the DH & PG employees, was in such bad condition that repairs might have been economically impossible.

A Government report stressed that in 1972 the total strength of WesternSamoa hotel occupancy had increased by only 20 double rooms. This was because of expansion at the Hideaway Hotel located on the other side of Upolu from Apia. This gave a total capacity of 175 rooms with 320 beds.

Nearing completion at the end of 1972 were 25 double rooms at Aggie's and 35 doubles at the Tiafau Hotel, located around the other side of the harbour from Aggie's. When the Tusitala opened this meant that there was a total of 332 tourist-standard hotel rooms in Western Samoa.

The report ended by emphasising "that tourism is expected to be one of the primary growth poles in the struggle for the development of Western Samoa."

In mid-April, 1974, when the 97-room Tusitala was officially opened, it was said to have cost about WS $1.5 million.

*   *   *

All Samoans, American and Western, were shocked to hear of the death of Prime Minister Mata'afa when he suffered a heart attack late in the evening of May 20, 1975.

Right from his beginning as the first Prime Minister of Western Samoa in 1959, Mata'afa established himself as a person of dignity and understanding. As the sad news reached the parts of the world where the PM had been received as a most respected ambassador of his country, tributes and messages of sympathy poured into Apia, including one from Queen Elizabeth and Prince Philip.

Since the establishment of the position of Prime Minister, Mata'afa had been in office for 13 of the 16 years — a remarkable achievement in a newly independent country.

Tupua Tamasese Lealofi, Prime Minister from 1970-1973 and who was Minister for Justice in Mata'afa's cabinet, was sworn in as caretaker PM only four hours after his death.

In March, 1976, the 47-member Parliament elected Tupuola Taisi Efi, 38, as Prime Minister by a decisive majority of 31 votes to 16.

Son of the late joint Head of State, Tupua Tamasese Mea'ole, Tupuola had been appointed to the highest political post in Western Samoa. He was familiar with the principles of independence, and the age-old traditions of the *Mau* movement through his grandfather, O. F. Nelson. Tupuola seemed assured of a long and valuable career as the Prime Minister of Western Samoa.

Polynesian Airlines' monopoly of the Apia-Pago route for 15 years came to an end in August, 1975, when Pago-based South Pacific Island Airways acquired reciprocal rights. The new operator was to use light aircraft such as Britten-Norman Islander,

Cessna, and in the future expected to acquire a 20-passenger *Twin Otter*.

SPIA announced that they would not affect the regular traffic carried by PAL but would generate and encourage a new clientele. This despite the fact they were compelled to charge the same fares as PAL and to fly a scheduled service between the two Samoas.

*   *   *

Commenting on the economy of the country at that time the board of the Bank of Western Samoa stressed the need for a growth in tourism. They considered that entry permits should be for a longer period than the present three days. Generally speaking the tourist industry was right behind the move to extend the 72-hour visitor-visa to at least seven days. No country could satisfactorily promote tourism as an aid to economy when the permitted stay was so short.

It wasn't long before stays of one week were granted. In fact, genuine applicants could extend their permitted time without difficulty.

Some years ago Aggie's Hotel would regularly employ a dance party from a nearby village — Matautu. Gradually Alan's wife, Marina, trained the hotel staff to do Samoan dance routines so that Aggie's dancers and the village dancers would appear on different nights.

With the village dancers there was Annette, a *fa'afafine*, also referred to in Samoa as "half and half". He/she was an expert dancer and was unquestionably the leader of the troupe. All the village dancers were girls, except Annette who started quite young as a star performer. As he grew up he became well-endowed and was the centre of attraction, especially with the tourist audience, the largest majority of whom thoroughly enjoyed watching, they thought, a Polynesian girl dancing bare-topped.

Naturally Annette was the target of many flashlight photographs at every performance. It was only the local people and a few regular overseas guests who were aware that Annette was a man — a female impersonator.

As Annette grew more and more appealing to many of the male tourists, Aggie was worried that her star attraction might be looked upon with disfavour by some, so she had Annette wear brassieres whenever he appeared at the hotel *fiafia*.

Annette became very popular, earning a lot of money dancing at private parties and other functions around Apia and in Pago Pago. Since 1975 Annette, who took a more appropriate stage name of Tanya, has been appearing at Honolulu night spots with great success. Once or twice he has returned to Samoa to see the village people. During the past twenty years Annette must be regarded as one of the best dancers to have appeared at Aggie's.

I spoke with Aggie concerning the time that Marlon Brando stayed in Apia. She said he came from Tahiti with his lady friend, a Tahitian girl, for a holiday in Samoa and stayed at the hotel.

"Unfortunately, he was so well-known that whenever he walked outside in the street he was instantly mobbed by Samoans who are renowned for their love of movies," said Aggie. "After suggestions that he should dress plainly to look more like a local, he decided to wear a T-shirt and ordinary slacks. In this way he did not attract nearly as much attention. But whenever he had the Tahitian girl with him the secret of his identity was given away. At one time he wore a *lavalava* to avoid detection but this ruse was also unsuccessful."

Aggie thought Brando was a wonderful person and he always took a delight in calling her "mother".

Aggie still has a few little "secrets" around the hotel to remind her of the past. Several times a day every guest goes by one of them. There is a short flight of stairs from Aggie's bar on the ground floor leading up to the office and the dining room. On each side of the steps there are iron handrails. At the bottom of one of the rails, the upright post section, there is a considerable dent or bend which has been that way for maybe twenty years.

"It was caused," Aggie told me, "when a truck accidentally reversed back. Had it not been for the handrail support, probably the truck would have been half-way up the stairs into the dining room."

In memory of the incident Aggie has never had the dent removed so it is there for all to see today.

Although the major additions to the hotel were completed in 1973, Aggie has refurbished and built several luxury *fales* for guests. This additional accommodation brought to 214 the number of people able to stay at Aggie's.

The extensive complex covers about three acres of beautifully landscaped tropical gardens surrounding the hotel units.

Travel agents offering passages on luxury ships often stress as a selling gimmick evidence that there are almost as many crew as there are passengers. Statistics of this kind are seldom ever applied to hotels. So it is just another unique feature of Aggie's that there are 120 staff to serve the 214 guests.

More and more Europeans are finding their way to Samoa. The varied nationalities can almost be likened to the influx of *papalagi* a century ago. Only then the visitors came by ship and stayed. Nowadays they arrive and return by air to their families in England, Western Germany, Italy, France, Switzerland, Sweden, Australia, New Zealand, Japan, the USA and Canada to name only a few of their homelands.

In the early 1960s organised island tours of Samoa were almost non-existent. Tourists had to do their own planning. As the international rent-a-car companies had not come to Apia, taxis were practically the only way to see the country. Frequently their charges were exorbitant and the service bad.

Aggie realised this state of affairs did not help her campaign to bring visitors to Samoa, and decided to rectify the problem.

For more than a decade now Anna Stancil has been associated with the promotion of tourism at Aggie's — in every way it's proved a good association.

Anna manages Samoa Scenic Tours and knows every nook and cranny of the country. If it is a trip around the island, a visit to Savai'i, or just a leisurely look at interesting and historic sights, Anna can make the arrangements quickly and efficiently — and with a happy smile.

Tourists are able to have Anna meet them at the airport, and this is a splendid way to begin a Samoan holiday. Anna's address is care of Aggie Grey's where she is located right in the lobby.

Alan capably manages the hotel for his mother so quietly and efficiently that the average guest would never know he existed. Everything operates so smoothly at Aggie's that there is never a necessity to call for the manager.

Each day from his top floor office at the back of Aggie's Store, Alan allocates the rooms and handles the complicated buying needed to provision a 200-guest tropical hotel. It is an unenviable task because so much has to be imported from New Zealand, Australia and America. Difficulties occur frequently in remote areas like Samoa with overseas shipping often unreliable and sometimes non-existent for months on end.

Always Alan has to be sure his freezers have sufficient meat, dairy produce and certain vegetables to last for several months in case ships fail to arrive.

With a day beginning at 5 a.m. he nevertheless finds the time and energy to do an evening jog around Apia Park. Even more surprising, Alan is able to effectively coach a football team during the winter months, and usually his boys finish the season as the Apian champions.

Alan may be quiet and unobtrusive but he has his finger right on the pulse controlling Aggie's Hotel. Every barbecue and *fiafia* night Alan will be at the guest *fale*. If you see him enjoying a drink with visitors, it would be a mistake to believe he is oblivious to the surroundings. Alan is not missing anything. He will constantly direct the Samoan waiters to this or that guest, ensuring that everything is aimed towards maintaining the outstanding service which is their reputation.

Aggie loves to dance — her graceful *siva* is a pleasure to see. In recent years Aggie seems happier than ever. She meanders amongst the guests, enjoying every opportunity to talk with these friendly people from so many distant parts of the world.

It's difficult to say who gets the greatest enjoyment when Aggie greets her guests at the *fiafia*. The legend of Aggie and her hotel's fame has now spread far and wide throughout the world. Of course it hasn't always been like this. Nowadays when many travel brochures glamorise holiday locations out of all reality it is a relief for tourists to arrive in Samoa and realise all that they have read of Aggie's renowned hospitality is true.

It is only natural that they should wish to see Aggie, to talk with her, to photograph her doing a *siva*, to learn all about her.

While guests may not notice Alan on *fiafia* nights, they will have no excuse for not seeing his glamorous wife, Marina.

Alan married Marina, daughter of Peter Thompson in 1960. They have three children, Aggie, Tanya, and Frederick, all the apple of grandma's eye. If there's ever a reason for Aggie not going on her yearly pilgrimage to New Zealand then it will surely be these grandchildren. Leaving them in Samoa gets harder and harder each Christmas.

Marina's father was one of those interesting people you meet in the South Seas. Like so many others Peter Thompson jumped ship in Apia, lured by the island life and the hope of prosperity and happiness.

With her training of the hotel's dancers Marina has achieved amazing results, particularly in recent years. The girls and boys obviously love every minute of their performances at the *fiafia*. They dance for the joy of dancing and a lot of this exuberance must be attributed to Marina's way of instructing them.

Guests will nearly always see Marina do a Samoan *siva* on *fiafia* nights, and sometimes daughters Aggie and Tanya. As can be well imagined it's a rare treat if you see these three, plus mine host Aggie, making one of her regular appearances.

One of Western Samoa's most important social occasions was the visit of Queen Elizabeth II during her world-wide Silver Jubilee tour. Accompanied by the Duke of Edinburgh, Her Majesty was accorded a grand reception in mid-January 1977 when she arrived in the Royal Yacht *Britannia*.

"The visit by the Queen was a really memorable occasion in our history," Aggie said. "Adults and children thoroughly enjoyed their opportunity to see such an important person. Hundreds of children lined the streets waving tiny Union Jacks. I'm sure the Royal couple appreciated the welcome they received in Apia. I had a very good view of the Queen as they drove past us on Beach Road."

A visit had been arranged to Vailima and to Mulinu'u interspersed with a lavish luncheon of typical Samoan foods — fish, *taro*, *palusami*, pigeon and even some *palolo*. During her stay the Queen was presented with a $100 gold proof coin specially struck by Western Samoa to commemorate the Silver Jubilee and her visit to their country.

*   *   *

While the Queen's Silver Jubilee was undoubtedly the most important international event commemorated in Apia during 1977, it is certain that Aggie's 80th birthday party was nationally the greatest celebration of the year.

Visitors came from many parts of the world — and added to these people were the hotel guests who, each year are always automatically invited to the birthday celebrations.

The 80th party outdid any festival previously held at the hotel. Aggie was her glamorous best and it was a wonderful occasion, October 31, 1977.

Aggie is a tiny lady by Samoan standards, about 5 foot 3 inches in her sandals. Despite her 80 years her sparkling blue eyes twinkled all the time, her lively expressive face had just a few wrinkles that were really only lines of happiness, for Aggie Grey positively exudes happiness.

The telephone began ringing early in the morning and shortly after breakfast the first of the well-wishers started to arrive. Aggie greeted them in her airy top-floor apartment overlooking the beautiful Apia Harbour with its cruising yachts gently swaying in the calm haven.

With windows flung open to the fresh morning air, Aggie's apartment had all the advantages of a Samoan *fale*. The cooling trade winds stirred the vases of freshly picked tropical flowers as Aggie greeted her friends with a kiss and a charming smile.

The birthday scene shifted from the apartment to a poolside morning tea. There Aggie was presented with a bunch of 80 glorious red roses, a gesture by Air New Zealand, flown from Auckland the previous evening.

Aggie, deeply touched by the presentation, did not lose any time responding with her renowned hospitality by ordering beer for everyone.

"It's my birthday," she exclaimed, "so even if it is only 10 o'clock — we drink beer."

Aggie entertained her guests at the poolside for several hours. There was a constant stream of well-wishers politely interrupting the outrageous stories Aggie gleefully told of the US servicemen of the World War II times.

For more than a week friends and relatives had been arriving in Apia — from America, Australia, New Zealand, and other parts of the South Pacific — all to honour the grand occasion.

Shortly after 6.30 as the sun was sinking, when the scent of the tropics is strongest, the guests began to arrive for the party. This was to be a night when the friendly elite of Samoa joined with the enchanted overseas visitors in celebrating in a way unique to the South Seas islands.

Aggie wore a glittering gold frock created in Samoa; behind her left ear was a bright red hibiscus. She looked radiant as she moved through the *fale*, chatting with guests, stopping at each table to exchange greetings.

"Thank you for coming," she said. "Enjoy your food, fill your glasses again, and dance."

The tables groaned under the plates and plates of delicacies cooked to a turn. The 600 guests consumed 12 suckling pigs, 150 chickens, 10 turkeys, and 10 hams.

For the Samoa appetites there was a mountain of marinated raw fish, 200 *taro*, lots of tasty seaweed, dozens of lobsters, and more than 200 serves of *palusami*.

At ten o'clock on that wonderful night Samoans sang a touching anthem as local people presented Aggie with fine mats, the highest token of their love and esteem.

In a gesture emphasising a quality for which she is renowned, Aggie asked her party guests to refrain from giving her birthday presents. Instead she said they should make donations to the Little Sisters of the Poor. Because of her kindly thought more than $3,000 was contributed that night.

The moment for which everyone was waiting came shortly before midnight. Aggie danced a Samoan *siva* as she had never danced before, her body swaying, her hands delicately telling a story with their movements.

Aggie was so happy, and the happiness was infectious. Guests jumped to their feet applauding and swarmed to join her on the dance floor.

It was past midnight when Aggie quietly left that fantastic party. She walked down the pathway leading to her apartment with granddaughters Aggie and

Tanya. Through the gardens of red hibiscus and the pink frangipani, under the tall swaying coconut palms and the overhanging green leaves of banana trees, just like any other night when the movies and the *fiafia* finished.

But that night had been so different. Aggie was 80 — so many memories would have returned, some long forgotten must surely have emerged, maybe only for a few fleeting moments.

It all had happened right there, at that exact spot on picturesque Beach Road where, in those early days, mountainous waves in Apia Harbour often tossed foam and spray on the facade of her little boarding house.

Forty years had passed since she began the long struggle with no money, only a grim determination to win — to be a success.

In that short walk from the *fale*, while the music from the band gradually faded into the tropic night, Aggie would have had many nostalgic thoughts — memories not only of the many difficulties, but also of the abundance of happy carefree times she has enjoyed in the islands.

From her modest beginning Aggie has reached the pinnacle of success. She is unquestionably the first lady of the South Pacific. Aggie Grey is a legend in her lifetime.

HONORARY Q.S.O. FOR AGGIE GREY

On 7 July 1983 the New Zealand High Commission in Western Samoa made the following announcement:

"Her Majesty Queen Elizabeth II has been graciously pleased to approve the appointment of Mrs Agnes Genevieve Grey (Aggie Grey) as an Honorary Companion of the Queen's Service Order for Community Service (Q.S.O.).

The Governor-General of New Zealand has advised Mrs Grey of the award and conveyed His Excellency's personal congratulations and those of the people of New Zealand.

The Prime Minister of New Zealand and Mrs Muldoon have extended their best wishes and congratulations on the well merited honour conferred by Her Majesty The Queen of New Zealand."

In his acknowledgments *Nelesoni* has thanked me for being patient when he was writing this book.

Really I didn't have to be patient because during his visits I have always enjoyed talking about the happy times and recalling the struggles we have experienced in Samoa.

Soifua

Aggie

Nelson Eustis first stayed at Aggie Grey's Hotel in 1958. This was before the days of the air service between American Samoa and Western Samoa.

With artist, Ted Roberts, he made the journey from Pago Pago to Apia in the *Sulimoni*, a small island boat well-known in Samoan waters.

Since 1958, during the course of his work in the South Seas, Nelson Eustis has visited Apia more than fifty times.

AGGIE GREY OF SAMOA

With numerous black and white illustrations *Aggie Grey of Samoa* provides a quick run down of Samoan history as well as being a memento of one its most entertaining citizens.
Pacific Islands Monthly

James Michener, who had cleared Aggie of the many unpleasant newspaper inferences concluded: 'She was a marvellous woman. I still love her!'
Sunday Mail

Woven into the biography are details of the Samoan Wars, the 1889 hurricane, the 1899 Berlin Treaty that split the Samoas, the Mau Independence movement, the NZ occupation, the 'prohibition era,' the 1902-5 lava eruptions, the impact of World Wars I and II on life in Samoa, and many other historical episodes.
The Samoa Times

Aggie Grey of Samoa is a must for all Pacific island buffs.
New Pacific Magazine

Her charms, her early life, her romances, her beloved mother Pele from Toamua, some of Aggie's secrets and wild stories . . . are all inside the book.
The Observer